THE ACADEMIC
LIBRARY DIRECTOR

THE ACADEMIC LIBRARY DIRECTOR

Management Activities and Effectiveness

JOANNE R. EUSTER

NEW DIRECTIONS IN INFORMATION MANAGEMENT,
NUMBER 16

GREENWOOD PRESS

New York • Westport, Connecticut • London

Library of Congress Cataloging-in-Publication Data

Euster, Joanne R.
  The academic library director.

  (New directions in information management,
ISSN 0887-3844 ; no. 16)
  Bibliography: p.
  Includes index.
  1. Library administrators. 2. Libraries, University
and college—Administration. I. Title. II. Series.
Z682.4.A34E9   1987   025.1'977   87-8375
  ISBN 0-313-25789-2 (lib. bdg. : alk. paper)

British Library Cataloguing in Publication Data is available.

Library of Congress Catalog Card Number: 87-8375
ISBN: 0-313-25789-2
ISSN: 0887-3844

First published in 1987

Greenwood Press, Inc.
88 Post Road West, Westport, Connecticut 06881

Printed in the United States of America

The paper used in this book complies with the
Permanent Paper Standard issued by the National
Information Standards Organization (Z39.48-1984).

10 9 8 7 6 5 4 3 2 1

Contents

Figures and Tables

FIGURES

TABLES

Preface

Does it really make any difference what library directors do? Is library management so situational and so constrained by circumstances that the impact which the individual director can have is minimal? As one visits academic libraries, even those reputed to be in disarray, one is struck by the fact that most continue to carry out routine library services, with or without leadership. The study that is the basis for this book, and the reflections and speculations that accompany it, do not precisely answer the underlying question. Nevertheless, I am encouraged to find that there are generalizable patterns of leader behavior and organizational outcomes.

Thanks are due to many colleagues. I am particularly grateful to the library directors who were willing to be the subjects of the study, who subjected themselves to the comments of their colleagues and sent me both encouragement and advice. Michael Buckland, Nancy Van House, and Charles O'Reilly were patient colleagues and guides. Dorothy Seiden provided invaluable advice about methodology. Sharon Euster spent endless hours tabulating data. Part of the costs of the research were underwritten by a fellowship from the Association of College and Research Libraries and the Institute for Scientific Information. Without the support and encouragement of these and many other friends and colleagues, this work would not have been completed.

Finally, but certainly not least, thanks are due to my husband, Stephen Gerhardt, who cheerfully forgave tennis matches forgone, movies unseen, and trips not taken, and who unfailingly offered advice, support, and encouragement.

1

The Role and Function of the Academic Library Director

This work asks and attempts to answer three key questions about academic library leadership. First, what is the state of leadership, within and outside of libraries, as reflected in the literature of the past fifteen years or so? Second, how does this and other literature of organizational behavior better help us to understand the role and function of the chief officer of the library? Finally, what conclusions can be drawn and recommendations for action made on the basis of this understanding?

The research study that constitutes the central part of the book investigates the role of the academic library leader, wearing her or his various possible titles of "dean," "director," or "university librarian," in influencing the external environment in which the library functions—the university environment surrounding the university library. The study focuses on four relationships:

1. How members of the external environment view the effectiveness of individual library leaders
2. How changes in the organizational domain of the library relate to the effectiveness ratings of the library leader
3. What activities effective library leaders perform in their relations with the library's external environment
4. Whether the level of professional and continuing self-development

activity of the library leader correlates with perceived effectiveness
or with changes in organizational domain

BACKGROUND

Failure of leadership is a recurring theme in library literature.
In 1972 Charles Martell asked, "Administration: Which Way—
Traditional Practice or Modern Theory?" and concluded that
library administration had fallen woefully behind in adopting
changes in management theory from the behavioral and organization sciences. Richard De Gennaro (1978) pointed out elo-
quently and forcefully that management theories were failures
in practical application, did not correspond to experience or
common sense, and diverted attention from the real issues of
administration. He concluded that management is an art, not a
science, and must be practiced as such. Charles McClure (1980b)
argued that "academic library managers have not provided
leadership in the solution of societal information problems, nor
have they effectively utilized innovative managerial techniques
to administer the library."

During the same period, Arthur McAnally and Robert Downs
(1973) reported on the uncharacteristically high turnover rate
among library directors. Their study of 22 directors who had
recently left their positions outlined ten environmental factors
exerting new or increased pressures on the library director and
recommended solutions and changes. However, they concluded that the characteristics of the "model director" re-
mained essentially unchanged; their recommended solutions
were primarily structural and technical.

More than a decade of such analysis and criticism has led to
some soul-searching; a broad spectrum of management workshops, courses, and programs; a noticeable increase in the
number of librarians who hold both the M.L.S. and M.B.A.
degree; and very little theory or research into what constitutes
effective or ineffective library leadership.

This situation is reflective of leadership theory in general. W.
G. Bennis commented in 1959, "probably more has been written and less known about leadership than any other topic in
the behavioral sciences." A survey of the literature concerning

leadership suggests that this is still the case, in spite of the proliferation of studies and theories.

The literature that will be reviewed in succeeding chapters reveals that there are at least two significant gaps in the understanding of leadership that contribute to this state. The first is the result of confusion between the concepts of leadership and management. The second has to do with the discrepancy between the rather broad concept of leadership implied in the articles decrying the perceived shortage of it and the quite narrow definitions applied by theorists and researchers. The first is rather simply explained, while the second will require more detailed discussion.

Library literature, like management literature in general, has tended to confuse the modern techniques of effective administration with leadership. For the purposes of this discussion, leadership will be defined as one dimension of the manager's work, the exercise of social influence. It should be noted, however, that while not directed specifically at influence, many of the other managerial tasks, such as planning, allocating resources, disseminating information, or monitoring work, also affect the ability of the manager to exercise influence.

The problem of conflicting understandings of the overall concept of leadership is more difficult. Examination of the literature of leadership theory and research reveals that the focus is almost exclusively on the impact of the leader on subordinates, primarily as individuals. Henry Mintzberg (1973), who has developed what is undoubtedly the most comprehensive typology of managerial work (to be described later), specifically segregates *leadership as influence upon subordinates* from all other dimensions of management work.

The discussions of failed leadership, however, are clearly asking for more than what might uncharitably be termed effective supervision. They are seeking behavior that will enable organizations to adjust to social and technological change, to develop meaningful goals, to design and implement the systems necessary to meet those goals, and to marshal the necessary resources. While a great deal of this process is the result of effective relationships with subordinates, a significant set of interactions is also required with what in general systems theory is called the external environment. Adaptation to social and technological change implies an understanding of the environment and the ability to draw resources for organizational change and survival from the environment. It implies complex exchange relationships with sources of funds and with those who determine policies and define regulations. It suggests dealing with perceptions as well as realities. The implied objective of leadership, then, is to infuse the organization with purpose and direction, to motivate members of the organization toward realization of organizational goals, and to influence positively the perceptions that the environment holds regarding the organization. Leadership is directed at realizing the twofold organizational goal: first, to create outputs of goods and services that meet consumer needs, and second, to acquire the resources and social sanctions necessary for the organization to expand and survive. While both goals may not apply to all organizations at all times, broadly interpreted they can be considered the end goals of both nonprofit service and profit-making organizations.

This model takes its concept of the organization in part from open systems theories and from the concept of strategic planning. In both cases, the need and ability of the organization to change are heavily influenced by the constraints and requirements placed upon it by the environment external to it. Thus, the organizational leadership must find some way of exerting influence inward, leading the members of the organization to hold common purposes and work toward realization of those purposes, and must also develop means to exert *outward* influence (not exclusively "upward" influence) conveying to the external environment the purposes, both present and potential, of the organization and obtaining the environment's understanding, support, and resources to allow the organization to move toward goal realization.

In the context of leadership literature, the exercise of internal influence is one of the primary tasks of leaders, although the bulk of the literature focuses on motivating subordinates and largely ignores the development of the overall mission of the organization. The literature on interactions with the environment describes the relationship of the organization to its relevant environments but does not address the issue of how the interactions take place. For the purposes of this discussion it is assumed that the leader or leaders perform the boundary-spanning role of concentrating the organization's outward influence and directing it toward critical segments of the environment. In the library setting, this means that the director seeks to influence members of the parent organization (university, city government, or corporation) to provide resources, to support expansion or contraction plans, and to accept the goals of the library as valid and thus deserving of support. Within the library, the department head seeks to influence upper library management in the same way. In the profit-making sector, the leadership seeks to influence consumers to acknowledge the worth of the company's products by buying them, to persuade bankers to lend money, and to convince government regulators and citizen groups to aid rather than hinder the enterprise.

Obviously, the interaction with the environment is not a one-way street. Models of open systems typically display the organization *reacting to* the environment and adjusting its outputs to changes in and feedback from the environment. Strategic planning models similarly emphasize environmental scanning in order to anticipate and react swiftly to changes in environmental constraints and demands. This flow of influence from the environment is considered for the purposes of this discussion to be a given. However, the exercise of *influence upon the environment*, as opposed to reaction, is also a key interaction and a major task of the leader role.

The study presented here first develops and then proposes a modification of the open systems model to take into account the dual function of the leader. In this model, the leader exercises influence, together with the tools of administration and technical expertise, on the organization and its members, who in turn produce the goods and services that are the outputs to the user environment. Simultaneously, the organization, through the leader, attempts to influence the external environment, which may also be referred to as the "control environment," in order to be provided with the conditions and resources that will enable the organization to achieve its goals. In addition, the organizational leader may attempt from time to time to persuade the environment to permit the organization to alter its mission and goals, the services it provides, or the media it uses to deliver them. This revised model serves as the foundation for the study of the behaviors and roles of academic library chief executives in influencing the library's external environment.

2

Related Research and Theory: Leadership

Several relevant bodies of theory and research will be considered in this discussion. First, there is the large, somewhat inconclusive literature surrounding the study of leadership in its many aspects. Second, there is the body of theory relating to open systems and the interaction of organizations with their environments. Finally, discussions of what constitutes organizational and leader effectiveness can offer direction to the problem of evaluating leader behavior. These three literatures will be considered in turn.

LEADERSHIP STUDIES

> There are almost as many different definitions of leadership as there are persons who have attempted to define the concept.
>
> (Stogdill, 1981)

Even though he implies that there has been chaos in the defining of leadership, R. M. Stogdill goes on to classify definitions of leadership into eleven categories. For the purposes of this discussion, these can be further reduced to four broad classes: (1) leadership as a function inherent in a group or organization; (2) leadership as an aggregation of personal qualities or traits; (3) leadership as effective administration; and (4) leadership as managerial style and behavior. A fifth approach combines many of the elements of the first four to arrive at a definition of leadership as the exercise of social influence in order to achieve organizational goals.

It is Stogdill's fifth definition, that of leadership as the exercise of social influence, that was used in the organizational and environmental model developed for this study, which will be described later.

Leadership as a Group Function

The earliest theorists described leadership as the focus of group activity and process. As early as 1902, C. H. Cooley stated, "the leader is always the nucleus of a tendency, and . . . all social movements . . . will be found to consist of tendencies having such nuclei" (Stogdill, 1974). More recently, A. Bavelas (1977) echoed the concept, describing leadership as an organizational function wherein the critical question is how leadership is distributed throughout the organization. To some extent, the concept of distributed leadership is reflected in current writings on participative management. Support for the concept of leadership arising from the group is found in the work of E. P. Hollander (1961) and others. Hollander studied informal groups in an attempt to discover the bases on which leaders were selected by the groups from among their membership. His study of what he calls "emergent leadership" is also used to explain the bases of power of leaders in formal groups.

Trait Theories of Leadership

Personality, or trait, theories of leadership developed in the 1920s and focused on the individual characteristics that enabled the leader to exert one-way, downward influence on organizational behavior and outcomes. Stogdill (1948) enumerated a typical list of leader traits:

- Sociability
- Interpersonal skills
- Social participation
- Activity or energy
- Self-confidence
- Intelligence
- Dominance
- Task knowledge

It should be noted that charisma, an aspect of leadership that is widely acknowledged, is not included in this list but was later described by the same author (Stogdill, 1981) as a function of a combination of cognitive, emotional, positional, and situational factors.

More recent theorists do not entirely disregard trait theory but focus on the questions of why and how individual differences facilitate effectiveness in leadership.

Management Skills as Leadership

Leadership as effective management appears to be the most common understanding of the term. Indeed, if all organizational outcomes are attributed to leadership, then it does encompass the full spectrum of management.

H. Fayol's (1949) seven management functions, referred to by the acronym POSDCORB, are planning, organizing, staffing, directing, controlling, reporting, and budgeting. Max Weber's (1947) concept of bureaucracy relied on the structure of the organization—the clear definition of each person's functions and reporting relationships—to ensure that the organization would function effectively no matter who occupied any given position. To Weber, the leader is simply the person at the top of the bureaucratic hierarchy, who has clearly prescribed tasks to perform. This explains some of the confusion and conflict in the literature. For example, the managerial techniques that R. De Gennaro found lacking all focus on methods that are designed to make the manager more able to *manage* effectively. Whether they are related to leadership per se is an-other matter. The explanation is that (1) leadership is one of many managerial functions but, in an apparent paradox, (2) management techniques of all sorts are at the disposal of the leader in fulfilling the leadership function. This paradoxical re-lationship is incorporated in the organizational model for the study.

Leader Behavior Theories

Leader behavior and style theories concentrate on variations on the two-factor theory first developed by E. Fleishman (1953) in the Ohio State University Leadership Studies. Two-factor theories utilize two dimensions to describe how leaders vary in their attitudes and behaviors toward subordinates. The "Initi-ating Structure" dimension describes the degree to which a leader emphasizes task behavior, and the "Consideration" di-mension describes the degree to which a leader emphasizes in-terpersonal concerns. The leader behavior theories reflect the earlier concern for personal traits of the leader but shift the emphasis to the attitudes and behavior of the leader toward subordinates. The Ohio State studies produced a number of widely used instruments for measuring leader behavior, sub-ordinates' and others' perceptions of the leader's behavior, and leader attitudes. While the instruments are the subject of some controversy (Morrison, McCall, and De Vries, 1978; House and Baetz, 1979), they are probably the most widely used of all in-struments for assessing leader behavior. A popular two-factor theory is represented by Blake and Mouton's (1985) "Manage-rial Grid" (©), which is used to give managers feedback about their attitudes and (presumed) behavior. The grid focuses on five major managerial styles, as illustrated in Figure 2.1:

- The high task/low concern for people style
- The low task/low concern for people style
- The low task/high concern for people style
- The high task/high concern for people style
- The central style, which represents balanced concern for both task and people

Figure 2.1
The Managerial Grid®

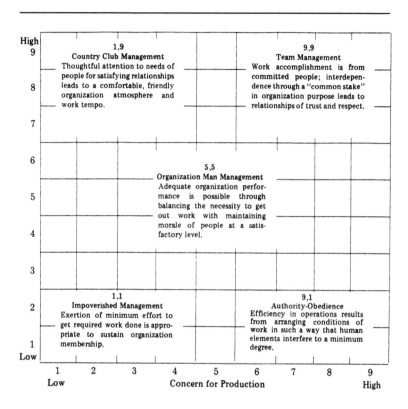

Managerial Grid figure from *The Managerial Grid III: The Key to Leadership Excellence,* by Robert R. Blake and Jane Srygley Mouton. Houston: Gulf Publishing Company, Copyright © 1985, page 12. Reproduced by permission.

Based on the individual's placement on the grid, the manager can assess personal strengths and weaknesses in relation to the particular organizational situation.

Situational or contingency theories of leadership draw primarily on two-factor theories of behavior, pointing out that no single leadership style is appropriate for all situations. V. H.

Vroom (1977) and his associates have developed a decision tree for assessing which managerial style can be expected to work best in each situation. The choice is based on decision-making behavior in specific instances; therefore, the style could vary markedly for the same leader in the same organization, depending on the decision to be made. The choice among decisions made by the leader alone, those made by the leader in consultation with subordinates, and those made by the subordinates as a group depends upon a number of elements: the time available, the need for group agreement to implement the decision, the need for information that the leader does not have, and, not least, whether the quality of the decision makes any difference. Other writers (House, 1971; Griffin, 1980) base effective contingent styles on task certainty, the technology of the work, demands of the outside environment, relative stability of the organization, and employees' social and personal needs.

Leadership as Social Influence

Formal authority vests the manager with great potential power: leadership activity determines how much of it will be realized.
(Mintzberg, 1973)

Many recent writers define leadership as a variety of social influence. The leader embodies certain traits, skills, competencies, and role behaviors that make it possible to exert influence on the attitudes and behaviors of subordinates. This definition does not exclude (and in fact builds on) trait theories, utilizes management techniques, and places a great deal of emphasis on leadership style and behavior. Hollander's (1960) studies led him to hypothesize that the leader is strongly influenced by group norms and values. To the extent that the leader is seen by the group as sharing social values and behaviors and being competent in work skills, the group will accept the leader. By virtue of this "conformity and competency" the leader will accumulate "idiosyncrasy credit," a sort of reservoir of good will and respect which the leader can then draw upon to act out-side the group role and norm expectations—which is to say that the leader can act as an agent of change, an innovator. Idiosyncrasy credit is a function of the group's perceptions of the leader's intellectual, interpersonal, administrative, and technical competencies and social conformity. The leader is both influenced by the group and able to influence it.

Jeffrey Pfeffer (1981) describes a somewhat different influence role for the leader. He defines the task of management as the provision of rationalizations and legitimations that make sense out of, and thereby explain, the organization's activities. *Organizational paradigms* is the term he assigns the set of rationalizations in which the organization believes. The tools of the leader in this framework are language, symbol, ceremony, and settings. The outcomes are shared goals, values, perceptions, and understandings. In other words, the task of the leader is to give the organization meaning and purpose in the eyes of its members.

The imposition of structure and goals and the taking of responsibility for the organization's basic direction are the principal functions of leadership, according to D. C. McClelland (1975). He defines this as the socialized face of power, wherein "the person is concerned to exercise power *for others*." McClelland and his colleagues designed and tested "power motivation workshops" to assist Community Action Agency workers in effecting social change among the rural poor in Kentucky. He identified abilities that enable the individual to strengthen the organization:

- Making others feel strong
- Building trust relationships
- Cooperating rather than competing
- Confronting and resolving rather than avoiding conflict
- Planning goals and steps to reach them
- Stimulating others to proactive rather than passive behavior

The leader's exercise of social influence includes mediating between the organization and the external environment. M. W.

Meyer (1975) argues that the function of leadership is "to mediate between environmental uncertainties and organizational structure." While Pfeffer (1981) describes leadership turnover, or "executive succession," as one of the symbolic events that help to maintain organizational paradigms, Meyer argues that stable leadership results in stable organizations because the leader is better able to protect the organization from environmental demands and externally imposed change. Two elements contribute to stability: leadership continuity and autonomy, which is defined as relative independence from external environmental forces. Meyer's construct is based on his finding that substantially more organizational changes occurred during periods after new leaders were selected than during periods without leadership turnover.

G. R. Salancik (1975) found that influence which leaders exerted on their peers, who were defined as other top managers in the organization, was related to their positions in the social structure, professional status and activity, job prestige, job variety, and social similarity to the other top managers. Influence on the external environment, which includes parent governing bodies and other units of a larger organization as well as the client group, is important because it is a major determinant of resources available to the organization. In open systems theory terms, the leader's influence on the environment mediates between the organization and the environment's perceptions of the organization's outputs, so that the consequent inputs are at an optimal level for the organization.

Management Role Theory

Mintzberg (1973) studied the actual work performed by five top executives. Based on his analysis of their actual behavior, he posited ten managerial roles, grouped into three categories:

Interpersonal roles	Figurehead
	Liaison
	Leader
Informational roles	Monitor
	Disseminator
	Spokesperson

Decisional roles   Entrepreneur
                                    Disturbance Handler
                                    Resource Allocator
                                    Negotiator

Mintzberg's definition of the leader role is rather limited. Although he states, "In his leader role, the manager defines the atmosphere in which the organization will work," he includes primarily supervisory activities as the actual tasks of the leader. Those primary tasks include (1) staffing—hiring, training, judging, remunerating, promoting, and dismissing; (2) motivation—giving advice, reassurance, suggestions, and attention to personal needs; and (3) probing into activities of subordinates—seeking information, intervening, and generally exercising "management by wandering around." Mintzberg adds to these three primary functions the warning that leadership actually permeates all of the manager's activities.

In the context of this discussion of leadership as the exercise of social influence, it is more appropriate to include all of the roles as leadership roles and to use the term *Supervisor* for Mintzberg's third interpersonal role. Social influence is central to all of the interpersonal roles. The Figurehead role requires the manager to carry out social, legal, and ceremonial duties because of formal status and position in the organization. The Liaison role calls for interactions with people outside the manager's own organizational unit. In addition, the informational and decisional roles include activities that contribute to the leader's repertoire of techniques for influencing both organizational subordinates and the external environment. The paradoxical nature of the interface between leadership and managerial activities is evident here: while leadership is but one of many management functions, those same management activities contribute to the ability of the leader to fulfill the primary function.

Leadership and Organizational Excitement

D. E. Berlew (1977) extends the framework for leadership behavior and effects on the organization, positing three levels of leadership, which in turn move the organization through four stages, from "dissatisfied" to what he terms "excited." Berlew's framework, illustrated in Figure 2.2, relates custodial leadership to the neutral or stable organization. The satisfied organization is the result of what Berlew calls managerial leadership. The excited or innovative organization is the result of charismatic leadership, which Berlew characterizes as personal influence exercised by the leader.

R. J. House (1977), in turn, builds on Berlew's framework to develop his theory of "charismatic leadership," in which he suggests that research hypotheses could be used to test his explanation of charismatic leadership. His theory is based on a set of individual characteristics that are reminiscent of those articulated by Weber, Stogdill, and others: dominance, self-confidence, the need for influence, and the belief in one's own values. In addition, specific leader behaviors lead the followers to respond: goal articulation, role modeling of the value system, personal image building, and communication of high performance expectations and confidence in followers. This tendency back toward emphasis on individual characteristics is shown in recent studies by David Whetten (1984), wherein effective leaders are described in terms of overall attitudes and behavior patterns, rather than in terms of empirically measurable attributes.

The Quest for Leaders

A significant number of books have appeared in recent years that have either a more popular or a more philosophical bent than the studies described so far. What these books have in common is their emphasis on the social need for leaders who lead—those who inspire others to action. Such books as *In Search of Excellence* by Thomas J. Peters and Robert H. Waterman (1982), *Corporate Cultures* by Terrence E. Deal and Allen A. Kennedy (1982), and *Reinventing the Corporation* by John Naisbitt and Patricia Aburdence (1985) express clearly what the authors see as the role of the leader in the organization and what the expected outcomes are.

James McGregor Burns, in *Leadership* (1978), developed a

Figure 2.2
Leadership and Organizational State

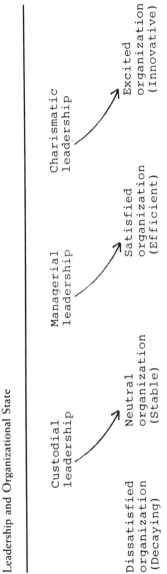

Charismatic
leadership

Excited
organization
(Innovative)

Managerial
leadership

Satisfied
organization
(Efficient)

Custodial
leadership

Neutral
organization
(Stable)

Dissatisfied
organization
(Decaying)

Adapted from Berlew, 1977.

complete philosophy of leadership, culminating in his theory
of "transforming leadership" in which the leader "looks for potential motives in followers, seeks to satisfy higher needs, and
engages the full person of the follower." Michael Maccoby, in
The Leader (1981), points out that old beliefs about leadership
and authority are no longer valid in the new self-oriented society. "The work ethic is not dead, but it has not been articulated for this age," says Maccoby. That articulation is the task
of organizational leaders.

In *Leaders: The Strategies for Taking Charge*, W. G. Bennis and
Burt Nanus (1985) further develop the theme of transforming
leadership, focusing on four specific behavioral strategies required of the transforming leader: having a clear vision for the
organization, communicating it so that it defines reality for the
group, developing trust among followers by choosing a direction and persevering with it, and self-respect and self-knowl-
edge, which engender self-confidence in others.

Leadership Studies in Libraries

Applications of leadership theory to the study of libraries have
been largely limited to use of variations on the Ohio State University two-factor theories.

R. Sparks (1976) reported an application of a version of
Fleishman's questionnaire to "the library department of a state
university." Both the leader and eleven subordinates were surveyed. The leader's scores on the "consideration" and "structure" scales were used to provide feedback to the leader "regarding employee attitudes, beliefs and feelings about his
leadership." Ways in which leader behavior might be changed
to improve the organizational climate and to initiate change were
suggested. Subordinates' perceptions of the leader's behavior
correlated closely with the leader's own perceptions on the
structure dimension, but there was divergence between subordinate and self-perceptions on the consideration dimension.
Examination of the actual response data for each of the 48
questions employed also showed that the leaders' self-rankings
were consistently in the mid-range of "often, occasionally, sel-

dom," whereas subordinates' ratings spanned the entire five-point scale, including "always" and "never."

A. C. Dragon (1982) administered the Leader Behavior Description Questionnaire, one of a series of instruments developed by the Ohio State University group to measure leader behavior and attitudes, to 28 subordinate groups totaling 166 individuals in three large public libraries. Subordinates in this study described their supervisors as being higher on the structure dimension than on the consideration dimension. In comparison to supervisors from other occupations, library supervisors were described as being as high or higher on initiating structure but lower than most in consideration. Professional and nonprofessional subordinates described consideration behavior similarly, but nonprofessionals described their supervisors considerably higher in initiating structure. The data were also analyzed by the sex of the supervisor, but no significant differences were found for either dimension.

Richard C. Holmes (1983) studied the library directors of a random sample of liberal arts colleges and comprehensive universities to measure perceptions of the directors' overall power in library decision making. Immediate superiors' and subordinates' perceptions were related to leadership style, role clarity, influence of outside groups on library decision making, and the directors' power bases. Perceptions of the directors' power over objective and policy-setting decisions were found to contribute most strongly to perceptions of overall power, and "expertise" on the part of the director was found to contribute significantly to the directors' power, as perceived by both superiors and subordinates.

3

Related Research and Theory: The Organization and Its Environment

Prior to the late 1960s, the study of organizational structure and behavior largely ignored the impact of the external environment on the organization. External forces were assumed as part of the understood circumstances but were not examined further. The implicit assumption was that the environment was relatively stable, and attention to organizational change was focused on efficiency and effectiveness issues. With the advent of the human relations school of management theory, the inward focus increased. Chester I. Barnard's (1938) theory of equilibrium emphasized the role of the executive as inducing workers to contribute their energies and talents to the organization in exchange for monetary and other rewards, but he did not consider the effects of other conditions in the environment.

OPEN SYSTEMS THEORIES

The organization as a system of inputs, processes, and outputs was adapted from theories of physical phenomena. Daniel Katz and Robert L. Kahn (1966, 1978) presented the most fully developed exposition of what came to be known as open systems theory. The model was refined to include feedback mechanisms, as illustrated in Figure 3.1. According to Katz and Kahn, the organization can adapt to changes in the environment in

Figure 3.1
Open Systems Model

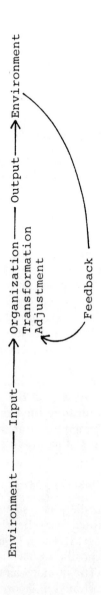

two ways. It can utilize a number of stratagems to attain control over external forces and thus maintain predictability, or it can develop internal modifications of the organization to meet the needs of the environment.

In the former instance, several methods of adaptation are open to the organization. It can attempt to gain direct control of parts of the environment, by incorporating those parts into the organization. Alternatively, it can design indirect methods of making itself less dependent on the environment. For example, it can build public support for its activities, create reserves of resources, or take advantage of larger systems in order to benefit from more powerful control mechanisms, such as laws or systems of social values. In each case, the organization attempts to buffer itself from outside influences. Thus the organization is able to assure legitimacy for its activities and gain protection from unfavorable legislation through its direct efforts and through the efforts of trade associations, professional organizations, trade unions, and organized lobbies.

James D. Thompson (1967) developed what is widely considered the definitive work on open systems theories of organization. He distinguished between (1) the environment as "everything else" and (2) the relevant "task environment," a concept first articulated by William R. Dill (1958). Thompson argued that each organization must stake out for itself a territory, or domain, in terms of its product or services, its methods of delivery of them, and the population served. The task environment, then, consists of the customers, suppliers, competitors, and regulatory groups directly related to the organization's domain. Collectively, they constitute its task environment, which is defined as that portion of the environment which is potentially relevant to the goals the organization sets for itself and its ability to attain them.

ENVIRONMENTAL ADAPTATION

The open systems concept developed by Thompson, Katz and Kahn, and others clearly indicates the potential for the organization to cope with environmental uncertainty and with change. For example, the organization could make internal changes to fit itself to environmental demands. It could adjust its position vis-à-vis the environment in order to reduce its dependence on it. However, the bulk of investigation has concentrated heavily on internal adaptation, both generally and in studies concerning libraries. Three discussions of libraries and their interactions with the environment will illustrate.

Richard E. Nance (1968) developed a model of user needs and fund allocations. However, he dealt only with the in-library decision to make expenditures in a specific area, based on user demand, and did not consider the external decision to allocate to the library. Beverly P. Lynch's (1974) review of studies of academic libraries in their environments described only studies that dealt with internal responses to environmental pressures and in particular organizational changes as responses. Snunith Shoham (1984) studied the adaptive responses of public libraries to reduced resources and to changes in the populations served. She concluded that in regard to population changes, the libraries chose to adapt to the changing demand. Where the loss of financial resources was concerned, efforts were made first to restore funding, and, when that failed, internal adjustment took place.

Studies of organizational efforts to manipulate the environment for the benefit of the organization focus on cooperation, co-optation, and strengthening the organization's power position relative to other, competing organizations. Pfeffer (1972, 1973) considered the organization's use of the board of directors as a vehicle for dealing with environmental uncertainty and interdependence with elements of the environment. He found that the compositions of hospital boards of directors were positively correlated with the needs and characteristics of the hospitals for financial and community susspport and with the legal foundation of each hospital. He concluded that the organizations studied used their boards to co-opt or partially absorb important external organizations or interest groups. In another study, Pfeffer and Salancik (1974) found that the power of university departments, as measured by membership on important university committees and ability to obtain grant funds, was positively correlated with budget allocations over time, independent of work load.

Rich Strand (1983) describes several organizational strategies for manipulating the environment that extend the concept to include altering environmental attitudes toward the organization. Thus, the organization might seek to manipulate constituent demands and expectations through public relations, lobbying, or using court actions to play off one power group against another. More difficult is the effort to affect the "goal states" of constituents by changing the physical, social, or psychological circumstances vis-à-vis the organization. Even more sweeping, but most difficult, is the effort to affect the general cultural and economic environment by introducing entirely new technologies, reorganizing the structure of commerce, or changing the role of work in the society.

PUBLIC SERVICE ORGANIZATIONS AND THE ENVIRONMENT

These studies clearly show the two-way orientation of the organization in an open systems framework. On the one hand, the organization may make internal adjustments to respond to inputs or feedback from the environment. On the other, it may make efforts to insulate itself from the environment or to manipulate the environment to permit it to avoid internal changes. The classic systems model (Figure 3.1) makes no distinction between the end user of system outputs and the supplier of system inputs. However, it has been argued that, at least in the public service sector, there is some separation between the two. Michael K. Buckland (1983) refers to the separation of the supply mechanism from the demand mechanism, and Karl E. Weick (1976) points out the dilemma of what he calls "loosely coupled organizations." Loose coupling, however, has the advantage of permitting organizational change and adaptation to take place more easily than in tightly coupled organizations (Aldrich, 1979). Within the organization, units and subunits do not have to rely on change in the total organization for their own adaptive behavior. Loose coupling with the external environment permits experimentation with adaptive forms and behavior and lessens the risk of any single form of adaptation to the total organization.

Katz et al. (1975), in their study of government service agencies, utilized a model of behavioral and situational inputs to service "episodes" that affect the client's evaluation of the agency and ultimately the client support for the agency and the governmental system in general. However, the relationship between individual support and inputs to the agency was not specified.

It takes little imagination to extend our reading of the systems model so that the portion of the external environment on the left, from which inputs to the organization come, is not the same as the segment of the environment on the right, which receives the organization's outputs. In that case, the organization's relationship with its environment in regard to inputs, or resources, may be quite distinct from its relationship regarding outputs, or products. It then becomes possible to refer to the two sectors as the *control environment*, which provides resources, and the *user* environment, which receives products and services. The feedback from the user environment provides the organization with information on which to base product and service changes; the user environment and the control environment are loosely connected. Feedback from the user environment to the control environment may be weak or intermittent. In addition, the control environment and the user environment may have very different goals for the organization and thus judge the organization by very different criteria. The organization, instead of basing its internal adjustments solely on user feedback, also attempts to influence the control environment to provide resources and legitimation independently of user satisfaction.

THE LEADER IN THE TWO-ENVIRONMENT MODEL

What is the role of the leader in this model? Mintzberg (1973) segregates the "leader as supervisor" role from the other interpersonal roles and treats them separately. Leadership is exercised *downward*, toward subordinates, and the liaison function deals with relationships with *outside* organizations and individuals. Within the more common use of the term *leadership* the two functions are combined, and it is in that sense that the function of the leader is used in this discussion. L. R. Sayles (1964) reinforces this definition by essentially describing the leader as a middle manager by virtue of the interface function between the subordinate unit and its environment or larger organization. Katz and Kahn (1978) similarly discuss the two-way orientation of the leader, and A. K. Rice (1963) describes leadership as a boundary function between the internal and external environments. Pfeffer and Salancik (1977) emphasize the importance of the outward-facing role of the leader, pointing out that if one were to assume that effective performance bears its own reward, then internal management is of critical importance, but that if one accepts the point of view that organizations are coalitions of interests contending for relative advantage, then the "representational" and negotiating roles become the more significant.

Carrying our adaptation of Figure 3.1 one step further, the leader is placed in the nexus position between the internal organization and the control environment. As the model evolves, we find the internal organization's outputs to the user environment resulting in only loosely coupled feedback to the control environment. Consequently, the control environment's allocation of resources and the permission it gives to the organization to exist and carry out its goals are mainly the result of its perceptions of the general value of the focal organization, the degree to which it contributes to the parent organization's ability to reach its own goals, and its relative need for resources and support. A principal role of the leader (or those who perform the leadership role in the organization) is to influence how the control environment (e.g., the parent organization) values it and consequently allocates resources and roles to it. It is this function which will be examined more closely in Chapter 5 and beyond.

4

Related Research and Theory:
Organizational and Leader
Effectiveness

Within this model, how are leader and organizational effectiveness to be assessed? On the one hand, the quality of the services provided will be evaluated by the user environment as the measure of effectiveness. On the other hand, the organization's ability to persuade the control environment to support it is less a function of performance than of perceptions. Those perceptions, furthermore, are only somewhat influenced by actual performance, if at all.

ORGANIZATIONAL EFFECTIVENESS

There is little agreement on what constitute measures of organizational effectiveness. Symposia (Cameron and Whetten, 1983; Pennings and Goodman, 1977) on organizational effectiveness emphasize two points: first, that the study of organizational effectiveness is critical to the study of organizations, and second, that while there are many potential measures of effectiveness, there is little agreement on their validity or applicability. However, two criteria of organizational effectiveness reappear throughout the literature, while a number of theorists have attempted to synthesize a third position reconciling the other two.

The two predominant models of organizational effectiveness

are the natural systems model and the goal model (Kahn, 1977; Seashore, 1983). The natural systems model views the organization in the context of its environment and measures its success by the extent to which it maintains equilibrium with the environment. Equilibrium is defined as maintaining a balance between the output of goods and services and the inflow of resources adequate to assure organizational survival. The goal model focuses on the degree to which the organization is able to attain an "ideal end state" (Pennings and Goodman, 1977). Stanley E. Seashore (1983) maintains that this model works best if goals are viewed not as the inherent mission of the organization but as the goals of individuals related to the organization; thus, the attainment of goals is defined as the ability to respond to requirements of the environment.

Others have attempted to develop a third model that synthesizes the first two. Cyert and March (1963) introduced, and Thompson (1967) further developed, the concept of the "dominant coalition" of parties who are in some respect or other stakeholders in the activities of the organization. The coalition determines the consensual criteria by which the effectiveness of the organization is judged. Potential members of the coalition might include employees, suppliers, government agencies, customers, stockholders or owners, and so forth. Hal Pickle and Frank Friedlander (1968) added to this list creditors and the larger community interest. In addition, they defined effectiveness in terms of the overall value of the organization to society. They further attempted to measure the relative satisfaction of each "party-at-interest." They concluded, however, that "it is clear from the low intercorrelations among societal satisfactions that organizational success is not a unitary concept."

A modification of the open systems model was proposed by W. Richard Scott (1977), focusing on process and defining effectiveness as the ability of the organization to adapt to changed environmental demands and consequently to maximize the organization's bargaining position. Seashore (1983) concluded that in their information-processing and decision-making roles organizations can be evaluated in terms of the appropriateness of decisions made.

MANAGERIAL ACTIONS AND ORGANIZATIONAL OUTCOMES

Pickle and Friedlander (1968) extended their model of organizational effectiveness to encompass management actions. They described organizational outcomes as a function of management behavior, which in turn is determined in part by management ability and personality. In testing their sample of managers, they found high correlations of critical thinking ability and verbal comprehension with the levels of satisfaction of the seven parties-at-interest.

Karl E. Weick and Richard L. Daft (1983) defined effectiveness as the ability of the organization to interpret the environment, a function which they described as the primary job of management.

Gregory H. Gaertner and S. Ramnarayan (1983) propose a quite different view of effectiveness that also offers the possibility of directly relating managerial behavior to organizational outcomes. Their position is that "an effective organization is one that is able to fashion accounts of itself and its activities in ways which these [internal and external] constituencies find acceptable." This process of organizational accounting is separated into four areas: auditing, implementation, integration, and legitimation. Only implementation results in specific outputs. Auditing leads to general outputs, that is, overall productivity. Integration consists of internal framework-setting activities through which organizational management and decisions are conducted. Finally, legitimation is the process by which the organization demonstrates to the environment that its organizational goals and procedures are of value to the environment.

Pfeffer (1981), as discussed earlier, also argues that the primary task of management is to "provide explanations, rationalizations and legitimation" that make sense out of and thereby explain the organization's activities. His position is that management effects are primarily expressive or symbolic, and thus effectiveness cannot be measured directly by outputs, since the primary influence is on beliefs, attitudes, and commitment. Anne S. Tsui (1981, 1984a), in her study of 330 corporate middle managers, argued that being perceived by one's "constituencies" as effective is a valid and reliable indicator of good management.

LEADER AND ORGANIZATIONAL EFFECTIVENESS

Tsui and Kirk R. Karwan (1984) further extended Pfeffer's line of thought in an experimental simulation designed to (among other things) test two opposing hypotheses: (1) that managerial effectiveness on the part of the "executive leader," as assessed by a team of external raters, will lead to favorable organizational performance, and (2) that, conversely, favorable organizational performance will lead to favorable evaluation of the executive leader's managerial effectiveness. In this case, favorable organizational performance was defined as substantive outcomes, in particular financial success. Tsui and Karwan found that time-lagged correlations supported the second hypothesis and did not support the first, which is to say that positive organizational outcomes preceded positive evaluations of the leader. Drawing on the work of Pfeffer (1977, 1981) and M. M. Lombardo and M. W. McCall (1982), Tsui and Karwan pointed out, however, that symbolic outcomes—creation and maintenance of shared goals and meanings—may eventually affect the substantive outcomes of the organization, since their results also showed strong correlations between substantive and symbolic outcomes. In addition, their research showed that symbolic outcomes were shared by and affected not only members of the focal organization but individuals in other segments of the environment upon which the organization was dependent.

This shift in focus from disputed measurements of productivity and the like to emphasis on the meaning-creating roles of leaders is also supported by David Whetten (1984), who points out that in his studies of effective leaders he chose to look for "generalizations of distinctiveness," rather than seeking indicators of any specific definition of effectiveness.

A relationship between leader effectiveness and organizational effectiveness has been shown to exist, but there is not yet a significant body of research that defines the nature of the relationship or the direction of the interaction between the two. In the discussion that follows, it is assumed, following Tsui and Karwan, that the perception of organizational effectiveness by members of the control environment is a precursor of perceptions of individual leader effectiveness. Therefore, leaders who head effective organizations are perceived as themselves effective. In this context, the reputational effectiveness of the leader may be considered a proxy for assessments of organizational effectiveness.

INPUTS TO THE ORGANIZATION

Symbolic outcomes take on proportionately greater significance for public service organizations, where the feedback mechanism from the user environment is only loosely coupled with the control environment. As a result, perceptions of effectiveness, social value, and goal congruency become moderators of both the organization's and the environment's responses to direct user feedback. The control environment thus provides the resources necessary for organizational survival and evaluates the goals and methods of the organization in terms of its understanding of the symbolic outcomes, rather than substantive outcomes. Therefore, effectiveness of those symbolic behaviors of the leader can best be measured by inputs, rather than outputs.

Traditionally, inputs are defined as resources that the organization receives from the environment in terms of money, services, personnel, and other operational requirements. However, a less tangible but important input is what will be referred to as "organizational domain." It consists of the approval the control environment gives, either explicitly or implicitly, to the organization to define or alter its own mission, goals, scope of activities, and methods of conducting its activities or meeting its goals. Within the context of academic libraries, an illustrative list of domain issues might include but certainly would not be limited to:

- Use of remote storage for little-used books
- Introduction of expensive computer technology
- Expansion of the print-oriented role to include the collection of audio-visual materials or computer software

- Inclusion of revenue-generating activities in the library
- Shifting from salaried personnel to contract services
- Creating and operating an internal library personnel office, computing service, and the like in lieu of using campus services
- Ability to design separate library personnel policies and procedures
- Replacing bound back files of journals with microfilm copies
- Ability to define and implement rules and regulations concerning the user environment (e.g., loan periods, fines schedules)

Domain issues will be considered further in the following chapter.

5

The Model

The preceding three chapters surveyed the research and theory that were used in developing the model that will be described in this chapter. Elements of the model are drawn from the literature regarding organizational leadership, the organization in its environment, and organizational and leader effectiveness. The model will emphasize the role of the leader as an agent of social influence. It will place the leader's activities in the context of a public service agency environment in which the control and user environments are loosely connected. Finally, it will relate perceived effectiveness and the ability to manage organizational domain to the leader's social influence role.

When last we discussed the two-environment model, in Chapter 3, the position of the leader between the internal organization—the library—and the external control environment—the university—was described in general terms. We move now to defining the role of the leader in affecting the externalenvironment and the operations of the internal organization. Figure 5.1 is a generalized graphic representation of the expanded model. It continues to be a variation on the open systems model of organizational behavior described in Chapter 3, modifying Figure 3.1 to take into account the nature of nonprofit and service organizations. However, the role of the organizational leader is also highlighted and separated from the

Figure 5.1
The Leadership Role in the Two-Environment Model

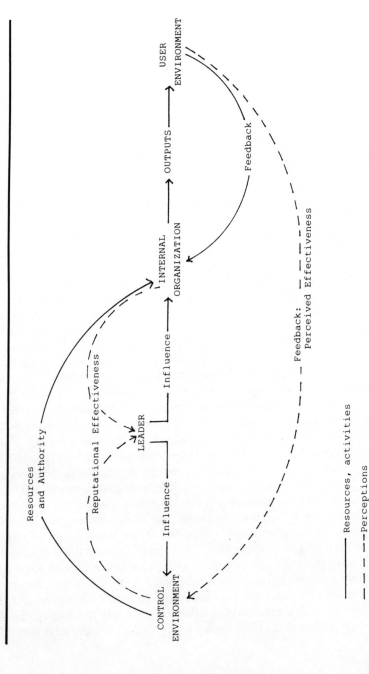

—————— Resources, activities
— — — —Perceptions

internal organization as a whole, so that the leader stands apart from the organization, serving as the principal moderator between the internal organization and the portion of the external environment that controls the domain and resource flow to the organization.

The feedback mechanism from the external environment, an essential element in the traditional open systems model, is altered in that the consumer, or the "user environment," is not the direct source of revenues or resources to the operating organization. Since resources are provided by a separate segment of the environment, which also defines what the mission, goals, types of service, and methods of delivery of the organization shall be, it is critical that some means be found to persuade the control environment to accept the criteria that the organization—the library—has set for itself and to provide the resources necessary for it to meet its goals.

Influence, of course, is a principal responsibility of top library leadership. In the model the influence function is shown operating in two directions—toward the internal organization, focusing upon subordinates, and toward the external environment, focusing upon maintaining and improving the library's position within the university. The self-regulating interaction between the organization and the external environment that applies in the traditional model is interrupted in the nonprofit service sector, where the feedback mechanism is less direct and is subject to interference and time lags. In libraries, countless surveys and studies are conducted to discover the level of service delivery, with or without also considering the user or nonuser's level of satisfaction, because direct feedback is clouded by value judgments about the various possible services (White, 1985) and because users typically do not pay directly for library services, or, if they do, they are often dealing with what is for all practical purposes a monopoly. For example, use of copying machines may be less an expression of satisfaction with the quality and price of the service than an artifact of the user's inability to remove certain materials from the library to a more satisfactory vendor. Conversely, user satisfaction with the library's services does not necessarily result in an increased stream of resources to the library. In that case, satisfied patrons may result in increased usage, but the necessary resources to maintain the service level may not be forthcoming.

In practical terms, the traditional open systems model may be considered to be the incomplete right-hand half of the complete environmental model in Figure 5.1. The choice of products and services, methods of delivery, resources for production—indeed, the very mission of the organization—are controlled by a sector of the environment that receives its user feedback through filtering mechanisms that are distorted by value systems, time lags, and vagueness. This sector, the "control environment," exercises its control on largely subjective and value-laden criteria. Predominant among those are perceptions of the effectiveness of the organization and perceptions of the relative value of the organization compared to other organizations under its control.

The organizational leader—in this case the library director—has a dual role. On the one hand, the leader exerts influence upon the internal organization, specifically upon the behavior of subordinates. On the other hand, the leader must also exert influence outward, serving as the principal representative of the organization to its control environment.

THE MODEL AND THE LEADER ACTIVITY STUDY

The Leader Activity Study examined the role of the top leader in the academic library organization as the principal source of influence directed toward the external environment. The environmental model from Figure 5.1 was amplified in Figure 5.2 in several respects in order to illustrate graphically all elements of the study. First, the generalized leadership influence characteristics shown in Figure 5.1 are based on the broad spectrum of leadership literature outlined in Chapter 2; in Figure 5.2, these are replaced by specific measurable activities:

- Managerial role activities
- Professional activities and involvement
- Membership on university committees
- Strategies for influencing the environment

Figure 5.2
The Two-Environment Model and the Leader Activity Study

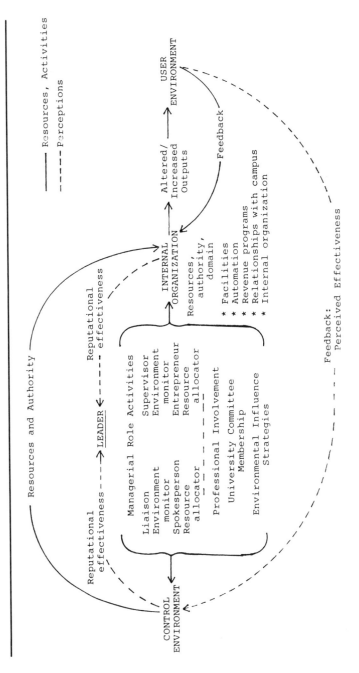

Second, the stream of resources and the authority granted by the control environment allow the internal organization to manage its domain and to grow and change as required by the environmental and organizational circumstances. Organizational change is defined as including five categories specific to academic libraries:

- Changes in physical facilities
- Introduction of major automation
- Introduction of revenue-generating activities
- Changes in relationships with other campus entities
- Internal organizational changes

Third, the perceptions that the control environment and the internal organization hold about the effectiveness of the internal organization and the leader are shown as "reputational effectiveness." Reputational effectiveness is the result of leader activities and is also affected by the indistinct feedback that the control environment receives from the user environment.

The amplified final model, then, contains the three major dimensions that made up the Leader Activity Study:

1. The reputational effectiveness of the leader. Because of the lack of clear feedback from the user environment to the control environment regarding the effectiveness of the services provided by the library, the perceived effectiveness of the leader is a powerful indicator of the perceived effectiveness of the library as a whole. The level of perceived, or reputational, effectiveness in turn becomes an influence factor in maintenance of or improvement of the library's position—organizational domain, in the model—vis-à-vis the entirety of the environment.

2. Managerial activities of the leader. The leader engages in a broad spectrum of activities that are directed toward both the internal organization and the external environment. While many of those activities are not intended as influence activities per se, the sum of them represents the visible efforts of the leader to maintain an effective organization and to relate it to the external environment.

3. Changes in the organizational domain of the library. The impetus for organizational change comes from many sources. New ideas are

generated, user demands change, the state of the art of librarianship evolves, national standards and systems dictate local practice, and personal styles call for changed structures. The ability of the library to implement changes, however, is largely dependent on permission given or implied by the parent organization, for example, the university for a university library. This permission may take the form of approval of and funding for major capital improvements, large-scale automation, or significant alterations in service patterns, or it may take the form of the explicit approval of policy changes or tacit approval in the form of the autonomy of the library to plan and implement change without seeking explicit permission, or any degree between these two extremes. Because of the rapid rate of technological and organizational change presently being experienced by libraries, it is assumed that change in organizational domain is the expected pattern.

The principal question that the study addressed is simply put: Are there relationships between the activities of library leaders who are acknowledged to be effective administrators and the degree of success that the library experiences in maintaining and altering its organizational domain?

The present state of organizational behavior research is equivocal regarding the relationships among organizational effectiveness, leader activity, and perceived, or reputational, effectiveness of the leader. This study helps to clarify those relationships in the context of the nonprofit service sector. In addition, answers to the research questions will help library leaders better to understand the importance and effects of their activities that are directed at influencing the external environment and will help them to evaluate their own use of time and effort on such activities.

6

Research Design and Methodological Notes

In the preceding chapters the relationships among individual leadership behavior, perceived individual effectiveness, and organizational effectiveness in service organizations were described in a single open systems model (Figure 5.1). This two-environment model assumed that the portion of the external environment receiving the outputs of the organization is not the same as the portion of the environment that provides resources and otherwise controls the activities of the organization. Feedback from the user environment to the control environment is generally indirect and indistinct. The role of the leader of the organization is to exert influence in two directions: toward the internal organization and toward the control environment. In the first case, the objective is to affect organizational behavior and outputs. In the second case, the control environment not only provides resources for the organization to operate but also defines what the mission, goals, types of service, and methods of delivery of the organization shall be. If the organization is to fulfill its mission, some means must be found to persuade the control environment to adopt the definition of domain that the organization has set for itself and to provide the resources for it to meet its goals. Lacking direct feedback of user satisfaction with organizational outputs, the organization must rely on its leader(s) to represent it and to exert influence on the control environment.

The amplified model in Figure 5.2 includes measurable and operationalized elements that constitute the dimensions explored in this study.

OBJECTIVES OF THE STUDY

The organizations chosen for this study are university libraries in the United States. The principal objective of the study was:

To explore and describe relationships between the activities of library leaders who are acknowledged to be effective administrators and their success in domain management.

In order to meet this objective, three principal research questions were formulated to reflect the three principal dimensions and the interactions among them. To reiterate, the principal dimensions were:

    i.   Perceived administrative effectiveness
   ii.   Managerial activities
  iii.   Domain management and change

The primary research questions examine the relationships between each pair of dimensions:

1. What interrelationships can be described between constituent groups' perceptions of the administrative effectiveness of the focal leader (i) and his/her managerial activities (ii)?

2. What interrelationships can be described between the managerial activities of the focal leader (ii) and the rate of organizational change (as a measure of domain management) in the library that he/she heads (iii)?

3. What interrelationships can be described between constituent groups' perceptions of the administrative effectiveness of the focal leader (i) and the library's rate of organizational change (iii)?

These primary relationships are then examined in more depth through two pairs of secondary research questions:

4a. What strategies and techniques for influencing the control environment do reputationally effective leaders in academic libraries employ?

4b. What strategies and techniques for influencing the control environment are employed by academic library leaders in libraries with high rates of organizational change?

5a. What are the professional characteristics of reputationally effective academic library administrators?

5b. What are the professional characteristics of academic library administrators who are successful in aspects of domain management such as making organizational change?

THE STUDY POPULATION

The unit of analysis was the individual organizational leader, also referred to as the "focal leader." The organizational leaders selected for study were directors of university libraries throughout the United States. The initial pool of libraries was the 105 university members of the Association of Research Libraries, which annually publishes extensive statistical data of its members, and the 86 additional libraries that participate in similar data collection and publication conducted by the Association of College and Research Libraries. Canadian universities were not considered for participation, nor were libraries whose directors were known to be in acting status or where the director had been in the position for less than one year. Further selection was based on geographic distribution, gender balance, and public-private balance. Large and mid-size libraries were chosen over smaller, although some smaller libraries were included in order to more closely approximate the desired mix of male-female directors and of public-private support. These criteria resulted in an initial list of 100 library directors selected to be invited to participate in the study.

The 100 directors were sent personal letters explaining the study and inviting their agreement to participate. Fifty-nine directors agreed to participate in the study. One element of the study required measurement of "reputational effectiveness" of the director, which is to say subjective assessments of that person's effectiveness as director by colleague and subordinate groups within and outside the library. Therefore, agreement to participate included agreement to allow those individuals to be queried as to the leader's effectiveness. These "constituent groups" included, for each university library, heads of Reference, Cataloging, Circulation, and Collection Development, and outside the library, deans of Graduate Studies, Business, Arts and Sciences, and Continuing Education. Where these specific positions did not exist, the nearest comparable position was used.

A response set was judged complete if questionnaires were returned by the director and at least one external colleague and one subordinate. Incomplete response sets further reduced the number of usable cases, and the final study is of 42 focal leaders. The following profile of the leaders and their institutions thus emerges:

University support:	Public	30
	Private	12
Sex of director:	Female	10
	Male	32
States represented:		30
Enrollment (full-time equivalent students):	Less than 10,000	14
	10,000-19,999	15
	20,000-29,999	8
	30,000 or more	5

DATA COLLECTION

The operational model (Figure 5.2) includes three principal dimensions: managerial role activities, domain management (resources, authority, domain), and reputational effectiveness. The Leader Activity Study questionnaire is a four-part self-administered instrument for the focal leader (Appendix A1) designed to gather data for all of these elements except reputational effectiveness. In addition, the questionnaire gathered data on use of specific environmental influence strategies used by the leader and on demographic and professional characteristics of the leader.

Part I of the Leader Activity Study asked the focal leader to report, on a five-point Likert-type scale, the degree to which he or she performed 40 activities that make up the following six managerial roles:[1]

- Supervisor
- Liaison
- Environment Monitor
- Spokesperson
- Entrepreneur
- Resource Allocator

Reported activity levels for these six roles constitute the measure of leader activity, or Leader Activity Score.

In Part II, the focal leader was asked to indicate on a checklist major changes that had taken place in the library during the past five years, or during the director's tenure in the position if that period was less than five years. Note that all respondents had held their positions for at least one year.

Part III concerned methods that the focal leader might use to influence the library's relationship to its external environment. These 27 items, prepared specifically for this study, are in turn indicators of seven major strategies for influencing the environment.

In addition to a limited number of demographic and organizational items, Part IV asked for a fairly detailed enumeration of the respondent's professional activity that was not directly related to performance of the job.

Reputational effectiveness scores were based on responses to the constituent questionnaire (Appendix A2). This instrument repeated the 40 managerial activity items from Part I of the focal leader questionnaire but asked the respondent to evaluate the effectiveness of the library director in carrying out those activities. A cover letter explained the study and the library director's knowledge of and agreement to participate in this process.

SCORE COMPUTATION

For each dimension, an index was computed on which to rank the respondents. Scores for activities in the six managerial roles were weighted to account for differing numbers of individual activities making up the role. Similarly, reputational effectiveness scores were weighted to account for varying numbers of constituent responses. Domain management, which was measured by the number of organizational changes that had taken place during the director's tenure in the position (up to five years), was also weighted to account for the director's length of service in the current position. Further notes on score computation are found in Appendix B.

NOTE

1. These roles are six of the ten described by Mintzberg (1973) and operationalized as item scales by McCall and Segrist (1980). In McCall and Segrist's factor analysis, the remaining four roles collapsed into the six that are used for this study.

7

Demographic and Professional Characteristics

What are the identifying characteristics of the academic library directors who participated in the Leader Activity Study? As a group, do they have educational, career, and professional characteristics in common? Demographically, who are they?

CAREER PATTERNS

Of the 42 directors in the final study population, 32 were men and 10 were women. The mean age of the group was 48.4 years, the median age 47.6 (Table 7.1). However, the women were on average 3.5 years younger than the men. The median age for women was 2.4 years less than for the men.

The directors had occupied their present positions for a range of 1 to more than 16 years, with a mean tenure of 7.5 years. The women's length of tenure was 6.2 years versus 7.8 years for the men, a difference of 1.6 years (Table 7.2). In terms of total number of positions held as a library professional, the number ranged from 1 to 11, with an average of 5.1, a median of 5.45, and a mode of 5.0 positions (Table 7.3). In all their professional positions, the directors had worked in as few as a single library and as many as seven, with both a mean and a median of four. The distribution of number of libraries worked in is quite flat; seven directors had worked in two libraries,

Table 7.1
Age and Sex of Directors

| | AGE | | | | | | |
	Under 40	40-44	45-49	50-54	55-59	60 & over	Total
SEX							
Female	1	2	6	1	0	0	10
Male	1	8	13	5	1	4	32
TOTAL	2	10	19	6	1	4	42

	Mean	Median	Mode	Lowest	Highest
Female	45.7	46.0	46	39	53
Male	49.2	48.4	48	39	66
All	48.4	47.6	48	39	66

Table 7.2
Number of Years Director in Present Position (Nearest Whole Year)

| | YEARS | | | | | | |
	1-3	4-6	7-9	10-12	13-15	16 or more	Total
SEX							
Female	3	3	2	1	0	1	10
Male	8	10	3	5	3	3	32
TOTAL	11	13	5	6	3	4	42

	Mean	Median	Mode
Female	6.2	5.0	4
Male	7.8	6.0	4,6
All	7.5	5.9	4

Table 7.3
Number of Positions Director Has Held

| | POSITIONS | | | | | |
	1-3	4-6	7-9	10 or more	No data	Total
SEX						
Female	1	6	3	0	0	10
Male	6	16	8	1	1	32
TOTAL	7	22	11	1	1	42

	Mean	Median	Mode	Lowest	Highest
Female	5.1	5.3	4,5,7	3	7
Male	5.1	5.4	5	2	11
All	5.1	5.4	5	2	11

seven in three, seven in four, nine in five, and eight in six libraries. Together, this grouping accounts for all but four of the directors. By sex the mean varied little, the men having worked in an average of 4.0 libraries, and the women in 3.8 (Table 7.4).

Professional education varied widely. All reporting directors held the master's degree in library science or its equivalent. (The M.L.S. equivalent includes all fifth-year postbaccalaureate degrees, including the Bachelor of Library Science when a fifth-year degree.) For 35.7 percent of respondents, the M.L.S. or equivalent was the only degree reported. Another 23.8 percent reported holding both the M.L.S. and a second master's degree, while 40.5 percent held a doctoral degree in addition to the M.L.S. Proportionately somewhat more women than men reported holding doctorates, 50 percent versus 37.5 percent of the men (Table 7.5).

These demographic and career findings roughly correspond to characteristics of the group of Council on Library Resources Senior Fellows studied by Dorothy Anderson (1984). The members of this group, while not all at the director level, were considered to be leaders in academic libraries or library education, since they were nominated and selected on the underlying basis of the question "Will this person be a leader in the profession over the coming years?" (Anderson, 1984).

Table 7.4
Number of Libraries Director Has Worked In

| | LIBRARIES | | | | | | | |
	1	2	3	4	5	6	7	Total
SEX								
Female	1	2	2	1	2	1	1	10
Male	2	5	5	6	7	7	0	32
TOTAL	3	7	7	7	9	8	1	42

	Mean	Median	Mode	Lowest	Highest
Female	3.8	3.5	2,3,5	1	7
Male	4.0	4.7	5,6	1	6
All	4.0	4.6	5	1	7

Table 7.5
Director's Level of Professional Education

| | EDUCATION | | | |
	M.L.S./B.L.S	M.L.S. plus masters	M.L.S. plus doctorate	TOTAL
SEX				
Female	3	2	5	10
Male	12	8	12	32
TOTAL	15	10	17	42
Percent of total	35.7%	23.8%	40.5%	100%

The mean average age of the CLR group of 25 was 47.1, compared to 48.4 years for the Leader Activity Study (LAS) group and 44.2 for a control group of Association of College and Research Libraries (ACRL) individual members utilized by Anderson. In both the CLR and the LAS groups, women were younger than men, by 3.0 years and 3.5 years respectively, versus a difference of 2.7 years for the ACRL control group.

The number of professional positions occupied showed similar correspondences. Female members of the CLR group had occupied on average 4.9 positions and male members 5.2 positions. In the Leader Activity Study both male and female respondents averaged 5.1 positions. These results differed markedly from the ACRL control group, where women had held 3.2 positions and men 3.5.

Professional education patterns were somewhat different among the three groups. Anderson reported that 60 percent of the Senior Fellows held second subject master's degrees in addition to the M.L.S., versus 39 percent for the ACRL control group. These findings contrast with the Leader Activity Study group, only 24 percent of whom reported second master's degrees. A different contrast appeared when holders of a doctorate were compared, however. While only 11 percent of the control group and 24 percent of the Senior Fellows held doctorates, 41 percent of the Leader Activity Study group held doctoral degrees. Female members of the CLR and LAS groups held proportionately more doctorates than did the males, fully 50 percent of the LAC women and 31 percent of the CLR women, as opposed to 38 percent and 17 percent of the men, respectively. In sharp contrast, only 1 percent of the ACRL women held doctorates, while 24 percent of the ACRL men did.

These similarities between a study of directors only and a study of a mixed group of directors and others in leadership and management roles suggest that in fact there are distinguishing career characteristics that set leaders apart from the general population of academic librarians. The relationships among some of those parameters and effectiveness will be considered next.

CAREER PATTERNS AND REPUTATIONAL EFFECTIVENESS

To what extent do the demographic characteristics of a library director's career pattern relate to perceptions that others hold of his or her effectiveness? Table 7.6 shows the relationships between perceived high effectiveness and six career variables. A moderate negative association was found between reputation and the number of libraries in which a director had worked. Low negative associations were also found between reputation and the number of years the director had occupied the present position, as well as between reputation and the director's age. A very low positive association was found between reputation and being male. In other words, the more libraries a director had worked in, the longer the director had occupied the present position, and the older the director, the less likely that they would be held in high esteem by their colleagues. On the other hand, male directors were slightly more likely than female directors to be rated as effective. The asso-

Table 7.6
Reputational Effectiveness and Career Pattern

	Correlation with high reputation frequency score (Pearson's r)
Years in present position	-.211 ***
Total positions held	-.010
Number of libraries worked in	-.367 *
Age	-.297 **
Being male	.109
Educational level	.037

```
*     p less than .01
**    p less than .03
***   p less than .10
```

ciations with educational level or the total number of positions held as a librarian are insignificant.

PROFESSIONAL INVOLVEMENT

The directors were asked to indicate a number of types of involvement in professional activities:

- Professional journals read at least every other issue
- Professional journals scanned at least every other issue
- National library conferences attended during the prior three years
- State library conferences attended during the prior three years
- Other library conferences attended during the prior three years
- Professional workshops attended during the prior three years
- Continuing education courses attended during the prior three years
- Other organized professional development activities attended during the prior three years
- The number of professional and scholarly associations in which personal membership is held (counting divisions of the American Library Association as separate associations)
- Committee assignments and elected positions held in professional and scholarly associations during the prior three years
- Papers presented to professional or scholarly associations or published during the prior five years
- Service as a panel participant or moderator at professional meetings during the prior five years

The number of journals read or scanned regularly varied widely, from none to 48 read and from two to 99 scanned. The mean number of journals read was 7.21, and the mean number scanned was 10.81 (Table 7.7).

The average number of national library or information science conferences attended was 6.24, with a range from none to 15. State conference attendance averaged 3.38, ranging from none to ten, and other conferences attended ranged from none

Table 7.7
Journals Read or Scanned at Least Every Other Issue

NUMBER OF JOURNALS	Number of directors in each category	
	Read	Scanned
None	4	0
2 - 5	15	12
6 - 10	18	18
11 - 15	3	7
16 - 20	1	0
More than 20	1	5
TOTAL	42	42
Mean	7.21	10.81
Median	6.07	7.75
Mode	6	5
Fewest	0	2
Most	48	99

(the modal response) to 12, with a mean attendance of 1.80 (Table 7.8). Since these figures are for a three-year period, the annual average rates of attendance are 2.08 national conferences, 1.13 state conferences, and .60 other library or information science conferences.

Attendance at organized professional development events was almost entirely in the form of workshop participation, with a mean attendance of 3.57, which is also close to the modal response of three. Seventy-one percent of the directors reported no attendance at continuing education courses, and 83 percent reported none at "other organized professional development activities" (Table 7.9).

Table 7.8
Conferences Attended (Prior Three Years)

| | Number of directors attending | | |
	National	State	Other
NUMBER			
None	1	3	18
1 - 2	3	6	15
3 - 4	6	24	4
5 - 6	17	7	1
7 - 8	8	1	2
9 or more	7	1	1
No data	0	0	1
TOTAL	42	42	42
Mean	6.24	3.38	1.80
Median	6.08	3.14	2.21
Mode	6	3	2
Least	0	0	0
Most	15	10	12

All directors reported membership in at least three professional or scholarly associations, and the maximum reported was
14, for a mean of 5.69. Committee membership and elected offices held varied more widely, from no assignments during the
prior three years to a high of 15, with a mean of 5.69 (Table
7.10).

Papers presented or published ranged from none to more
than 15 during the prior five years. The mean number was 6.31
papers, and the modal response was three. In addition to papers, the directors were queried about participation on panels
at professional associations, either as panelists or as moderators. They reported serving as panelists an average of 3.6 times

Table 7.9
Workshops, Courses, and Continuing Education (Prior Three Years)

| | Number of directors attending | | |
	Workshops	Courses	Other
NUMBER			
None	8	30	35
1 - 2	8	8	3
3 - 4	15	2	2
5 - 6	1	0	0
7 - 8	2	0	0
9 or more	5	0	0
No data	2	2	2
TOTAL	42	42	42
Mean	3.57	.48	.25
Median	3.17	1.90	2.00
Mode	3	0	0
Fewest	0	0	0
Most	17	3	3

during the prior five years, although the modal response was less, at two times. Moderator roles were less frequent, with the modal response being "none," and a mean of 1.33 (Table 7.11).

PROFESSIONAL INVOLVEMENT AND REPUTATIONAL EFFECTIVENESS

To what extent does participation in various professional activities correlate with the director's perceived effectiveness within the university and the library? High reputational effectiveness scores were correlated with the frequency with which the di-

Table 7.10
Professional Association and University Activity (Prior Three Years)

| | Association | | University-wide |
	Membership	Assignments	Committees/Task forces
NUMBER			
None	0	2	1
1 - 2	0	4	4
3 - 4	17	13	11
5 - 6	11	10	13
7 - 8	12	6	5
9 or more	2	7	8
TOTAL	42	42	42
Mean	5.69	5.69	6.07
Median	5.63	5.50	5.19
Mode	4	4	5
Fewest	3	0	0
Most	14	15	21

rectors read or scanned journals, attended conferences, attended workshops, participated in professional associations through membership or holding office or committee assignments, published or presented papers or served on panel discussions, and served on university-wide committees. A moderate negative degree of association ($r = -.481$) was found between reputation and attendance at workshops and classes. Table 7.9 had indicated that overall attendance at such programs was very low, with fully 83 percent of the responding directors having attended no workshops or courses during the prior three years. Since this activity is so seldom engaged in, conclusions based on the association would be speculative at best.

Table 7.11
Publications and Presentations (Prior Five Years)

	Papers	Panels	
		Panelist	Moderator
NUMBER			
None	2	5	17
1 - 2	11	13	16
3 - 4	12	16	7
5 - 6	6	2	2
7 - 8	3	3	0
9 or more	8	3	0
TOTAL	42	42	42
Mean	6.31	3.60	1.33
Median	3.75	3.11	2.00
Mode	3	2	0

PROFESSIONAL INVOLVEMENT INDEX

The wide range of professional participation reported for the twelve different categories was reduced to a single, more manageable index of professional involvement. The index is a simple summation of the incidences reported of *any* type of professional participation. No attempt is made to assign greater weight to one activity than to another. This procedure is similar to the technique employed by C. R. McClure (1980a) in which an additive score was used to describe the "information richness" of the librarians in his study. By weighting all professional involvement items equally, it is possible to an extent to take into account the different personal preferences, priorities, learning, and interpersonal styles of the individual directors.

The resulting Professional Involvement Scores are displayed in Figure 7.1. The range of scores is 28 to 169, with a mean

Figure 7.1
Professional Involvement Scores

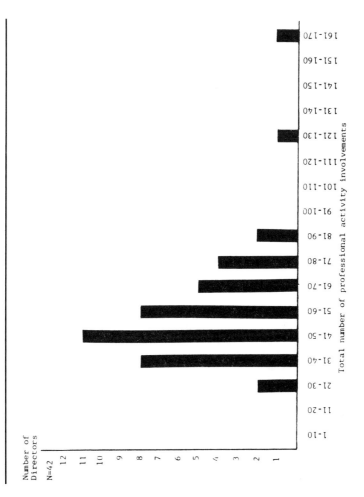

score of 56.43 and a median of 51.00. Sixty-four percent of the
scores fall into the range 31 to 60.

UNIVERSITY COMMITTEE ACTIVITY

The directors were also asked to indicate the number of elected
or appointed university committees they had served on during
the prior three years. The range of university assignments varied from none to 21, with a mean of 6.07 (Table 7.10). The
modal response was five, and 67 percent of responses fell in
the range of three to seven.

UNIVERSITY COMMITTEE ACTIVITY AND
REPUTATIONAL EFFECTIVENESS

While the association between reputational effectiveness and
the five individual categories of professional activity was weak
and inconclusive, a moderate positive association was found
between service on university committees and reputation ($r =$
.372). This association raises interesting questions. Does one
enjoy high esteem because of membership on such bodies? Or,
conversely, does high reputation result in one's being appointed to university-wide responsibilities? Speculatively, one
might conclude that the two characteristics are reciprocal, with
one reinforcing the other.

THE MODAL DIRECTOR

Aggregating the most frequent responses to each of these
questions, one can assemble the characteristics of a fictitious
modal (as distinguished from *model*) director. (Several distinct
models will be discussed in Chapter 10.) The modal director is
male and is 48 years old. He has occupied his present position
for four years and has worked in a total of five libraries, occu-
pying a total of five separate positions. He holds the M.L.S. or
equivalent plus a doctorate.

The modal director reads six professional journals regularly
and scans an additional five. In the past three years he has
attended six national, three state, and two "other" library or

information science conferences, as well as three continuing education workshops. He belongs to four professional associations and has held either four or six offices or committee positions in the associations. Within his own university, he has served on five university committees or other bodies. He has published or presented three papers to professional or scholarly associations during the past five years and has also served on two panels as a participant but not as a moderator.

The modal director differs from the *average* director in several respects:

	Mode	Mean
Years in position	4	7.5
Libraries worked in	7	4.0
Journals scanned	5	10.81
Association memberships	4	5.69
University assignments	5	6.07
Papers published/presented	3	6.31

In other categories, the mode and mean are closer, as shown in Tables 7.1 through 7.11.

Career patterns, involvement in professional activities, and university committee membership will be discussed in later chapters in relation to the three principal dimensions and the four model leader types.

8

Directors' Activities and Effectiveness Ratings

What do library chief executives actually do in performance of their jobs? Mintzberg's 1973 diary studies resulted in identification of ten managerial roles that are common to a broad spectrum of managers. M. W. McCall and C. A. Segrist (1980) created operational scales for six of the ten roles; in their factor analysis, the remaining four roles were found to collapse into the six primary roles that were used in the Leader Activity Study.[1]

The 42 responding leaders reported on a total of 40 items constituting the six roles—Supervisor, Liaison, Environment Monitor, Entrepreneur, Spokesperson, and Resource Allocator—on a five-point scale, in terms of the extent to which they engaged in each activity. Thus, responses ranged from "1—Not at all" to "5—To an extreme extent." The mean response for all items was 3.6, falling between 3, "To a moderate extent," and 4, "To a considerable extent." The average activity scores for each of the six roles are profiled in Table 8.1.

The extent of leader activity is of greatest interest in terms of how it relates to the leader's effectiveness in the performance of the job. Since the constituent questionnaires utilized the same 40 activity items, for comparison purposes assessments of the directors' *effectiveness* are profiled along with reported *activity* on the same scales in Table 8.1.

Table 8.1
Mean Scores for Managerial Roles

Managerial Role	Managerial Activity	Effectiveness Ratings		Score Profiles
		Mid-Managers	Deans	
Supervisor	3.13	3.06	3.68	
Liaison	3.77	3.83	4.13	
Environment Monitor	3.68	3.68	4.07	
Entrepreneur	4.07	3.44	4.01	
Spokesperson	3.72	3.79	4.11	
Resource Allocator	3.84	3.48	3.87	
All roles combined	3.60	3.48	3.93	

○———○ Directors' report of extent of own activity

○- - -○ Middle managers' ratings of directors' effectiveness

○·········○ Deans' ratings of directors' effectiveness

The highest single activity role, as reported by the directors, was that of Entrepreneur, and the lowest, Supervisor. Activity levels in the Supervisor role were lower than for all other roles.

In performance of every role, the deans rated the directors' effectiveness higher than did the library middle managers.

In order to test the significance of these observed differences, variance analysis was performed on the three possible pairs of perceptions—director/middle managers, director/deans, and middle managers/deans. No significant variance was found between the overall perceptions by subordinates of effectiveness of role performance and the directors' report of the extent of activity performed. When the same data were analyzed for each individual role, however, a significant difference was found between perceived effectiveness and role activity for the Entrepreneur role (at the .025 level). No significant differences between directors' and middle managers' perceptions were found for the remaining five roles.

The same analysis applied to the director reports of activity vis-à-vis the deans' perceptions of effectiveness revealed that for all roles combined, significant variance in assessments pertained, at the .005 level. Within specific roles, significant variance was found for the Supervisor, Liaison, Environment Monitor, and Spokesperson roles, while no significant differences were noted in the Entrepreneur and Resource Allocator roles.

These findings suggest that external peers may be evaluating primarily on the basis of observed results and only to a limited extent on the basis of the manager's activities directed toward those results. In addition, it is possible that extent of effort directed toward a given activity is not related to perceived or actual effectiveness in that activity. However, the presumption is that extent of effort and effectiveness are related. If there is a significant discrepancy between effort and effectiveness, the amount of activity may be misplaced or the way in which the activity is carried out may be inappropriate to the particular situation. The principal concern for effective management is that the activity is performed *and* that it is performed in a way suitable to the situation, so that maximum result is obtained at the least cost in managerial time.

Finally, the perceptions of the two colleague groups as to the effectiveness of the director in each role were compared. When the 40 report items were considered as a whole ("Overall"), the variance in perceptions was significant at the .005 level. Significant variances were also noted for five of the six roles; only for the Liaison role did perceived effectiveness match closely between the two colleague groups.

These findings support the assumption that internal and external raters will tend to evaluate performance differently. At the same time, the findings also reveal that the internal raters' perceptions of effectiveness closely match the directors' perceptions of their own extent of activity, while the external raters' perceptions do not correlate closely with reported activity. Two possible explanations are suggested. First, it is likely that library middle managers are in a better position to observe the director's activities and to evaluate results. Second, the middle managers are also more likely to be knowledgeable about the details of library work and can evaluate specific items more precisely, whereas the dean-level colleagues outside the library evaluate more impressionistically, basing their conclusions on overall perceptions of the effectiveness of the director. If, as this explanation suggests, evaluations are based on what each knows best, a corollary would be that the middle managers know relatively more about library activities but less about effectiveness, which is a more general concept and not subject to objective evaluation. Conversely, the deans, while knowing less about library activities, may have a better understanding of overall effectiveness or may be influenced more by symbolic outcomes.

In the two cases where the middle managers' ratings vary significantly from the leaders' reported activity—the Spokesperson and Entrepreneur roles—the items making up the role are primarily externally oriented, which would make it more difficult for the internal raters to have direct observational information. The Resource Allocator role is the single instance in which, overall, both the deans' and the subordinates' perceptions of role performance matched the directors' report of the extent of activity fairly closely. One possible explanation is that resource allocation is an activity that is better documented than most, and therefore both activity and outcomes can be assessed on physical evidence, as opposed to subjective evaluations of other managerial activities.

INDIVIDUAL ACTIVITIES

Each of the six managerial role scores was the result of combining responses to a number of listed individual activities. Examination of the individual activities constituted the final level of activity and effectiveness analysis. Again, the mean activity scores of the directors were compared to the effectiveness ratings assigned by the middle managers and the deans. These comparisons are displayed as Activity/Effectiveness Profiles for each role in Tables 8.2 through 8.7.

It is presumed that if the manager is expending a great deal of effort on an activity yet is rated as performing that activity at a lower effectiveness level, the amount of activity may be misplaced or the techniques employed not appropriate to the specific organizational situation.

Five activity items were identified where one of the rater groups assessed effectiveness at least .6 points lower than the mean activity level reported by the directors. All of the lower ratings were assigned by middle managers, none by deans. The items were:

1. Evaluating subordinate job performance (Supervisor)
6. Forwarding important information to subordinates (Supervisor)
31. Staying attuned to informal communication networks of the university (Liaison)
17. Solving problems by instituting needed changes in the library (Entrepreneur)
40. Obtaining adequate resources to administer library service programs and build library collections (Resource Allocator)

Three explanations for these discrepancies in effort and effectiveness can be proposed. First, it is possible that the managers tended to rate themselves more highly on these items than on other items. The directors did in fact report activity levels higher than their own mean activity levels for each role for items 1

Table 8.2
Activity/Effectiveness Profile, Supervisor Role

Score Profiles

Activity Item

Evaluating subordinate job performance

Integrating subordinates' goals with the library's goals and objectives

Forwarding important information to subordinates

Directing the work of subordinates

Allocating human resources to tasks

Resolving conflicts between subordinates

Relating subordinates' skills and job assignments to facilitate growth

Giving critical negative feedback

Alerting subordinates to problems

Using authority to insure that tasks are done

Providing new employees with training

O————O Directors' report of extent of own activity

O— — —O Middle managers' ratings of directors' effectiveness

O·········O Deans' ratings of directors' effectiveness

Table 8.3
Activity/Effectiveness Profile, Liaison Role

Score Profiles

Activity Item	2	3	4	5

Attending university social functions for contacts

Attending conferences or meetings

Representing the library at social functions

Staying attuned to informal communication networks

Developing contacts with people outside the library

○———○ Directors' report of extent of own activity

○- - -○ Middle managers' ratings of directors' effectiveness

○·······○ Deans' ratings of directors' effectiveness

Table 8.4
Activity/Effectiveness Profile, Environment Monitor Role

Score Profile

Activity Item

Initiating new ideas for services and operations

Keeping up with professional trends and changes

Keeping up with information on the progress of
programs and operations throughout the university

Keeping up with technological developments

Scanning the environment for new opportunities to
improve services or operations

Gathering information about users, the university,
new professional developments

Touring facilities or workstations to observe

Learning about new ideas from outside the library

Reading reports of other units of the university

O————O Directors' report of extent of own activity

O————O Middle managers' ratings of directors' effectiveness

O·······O Deans' ratings of directors' effectiveness

Table 8.5
Activity/Effectiveness Profile, Entrepreneur Role

Score Profiles

Activity Item

Planning and implementing changes in the
    library

Initiating controlled change in the library

Solving problems by instituting needed changes
    in the library

O————O Directors' report of extent of own activity

O— — —O Middle managers' ratings of directors' effectiveness

O·······O Deans' ratings of directors' effectiveness

73

Table 8.6
Activity/Effectiveness Profile, Spokesperson Role

Activity Item	Score Profiles

Serving as an expert or advising people
outside the library

Keeping others informed of the library's plans

Answering letters or inquiries on behalf of
the library

Serving on committees, representing the library

Providing other people with information about the
library's activities and plans

⊶——⊶ Directors' report of extent of own activity

⊶– –⊶ Middle managers' ratings of directors' effectiveness

○········○ Deans' ratings of directors' effectiveness

74

Table 8.7
Activity/Effectiveness Profile, Resource Allocator Role

Activity Item

Distributing budgeted resources

Making decisions about time parameters for
upcoming programs

Preventing the loss of human or capital resources

Allocating monies within the library

Deciding which programs to provide resources to

Allocating equipment or materials

Obtaining adequate resources to administer
library programs and build collections

Score Profiles

o————o Directors' report of extent of own activity

o— — —o Middle managers' ratings of directors' effectiveness

o·········o Deans' ratings of directors' effectiveness

75

(evaluating subordinates), 6 (forwarding information), and 40 (obtaining adequate resources). On the other hand, reported activity levels for items 17 (instituting changes) and 31 (informal communication networks) were close to the mean activity score for each role.

A second possible explanation is that for the first five items, the nature of the activity is such that subordinates will always want or expect greater results than can reasonably be delivered. Intuitively, this is a likely situation for items 6 (forwarding information) and 40 (obtaining adequate resources) but less so for the remaining items.

The third possibility is that these items do not represent appropriate tasks for the top executive in the library organization. However, given that the activity items had been previously validated and were based on Mintzberg's initial diary studies, this seems unlikely. Furthermore, one must ask, if this were indeed the case, why had the directors reported at least average activity levels on all five items?

Finally, it should be noted that this level of analysis is very close to the anecdotal, consisting of simple examination of data rather than statistical analysis.

Utilization of specific strategies for influencing the external environment is a technique which is more goal-focused than are the individual items and roles that constitute leader activity. The yes/no checklist of use of external influence strategies that constituted Part III of the Leader Activity Study yielded a very high number of "yes" responses. Overall utilization of the 27 strategic items was reported at 77 percent of all possible positive responses, with a fairly narrow range of 60 percent to 90 percent utilization. This finding indicates that the directors as a group are highly oriented toward generalized goals, an orientation that appears to be respected by their peers outside the libraries.

NOTE

1. The four roles that were eliminated are Figurehead, Disseminator, Disturbance Handler, and Negotiator. See also note to Chapter 6.

9

Organizational Change

The ability of the library to manage its own "organizational domain" is critical to its survival. Obviously, the flow of resources from the university is vital. However, of equal and perhaps greater significance is the ability to decide what services and programs to implement in order to fulfill the library's mission, the ability to select the methods of delivering services, and the autonomy to organize the library to carry out its programs effectively. In short, along with resources, domain management must include the authority to utilize resources effectively.

The rate of change that a library experiences is one measure of management of organizational domain. The Leader Activity Study asked the library directors to identify which among five categories of organizational changes had occurred in their libraries during the past five years or during their appointments as director, whichever time was shorter. The five categories are listed in rank order of the frequency of their occurrence among the libraries:

1. Introduction of major library automation projects, including circulation, public catalogs, acquisitions, cataloging support, serials control, and automated document delivery (occurrence index, weighted by number of years of the director's tenure, 22)
2. Changes in the internal organization of the library, including changes

in organizational structure and staffing patterns, and the addition or discontinuance of collections or services (occurrence index, 21)

3. Changes in library facilities, including planning or construction of new buildings, additions or renovations and introduction of compact or remote storage, or microform storage (occurrence index, 19)

4. Changes in relationships with other campus entities, including relationships with computing services, central personnel offices, and faculty (occurrence index, 18)

5. Introduction of revenue-generating activities in the library, such as on-line bibliographic services, copying, or sales of publications for cost recovery or profit (occurrence index, 15)

As can be seen, changes associated with library automation occurred most frequently, followed closely by internal organizational changes, while the least frequently reported changes involved introduction of revenue-generating activities within the libraries. To test the significance of differences in reported frequencies of changes, a chi-square analysis of expected and actual frequencies of each type of change was performed, and the variation in patterns of change was found to be significant at the .05 level.

On the whole, it is not unlikely that some categories of change would be introduced more or less frequently than would be expected by a simple uniform distribution. First, many internal organizational changes can be accomplished at a relatively low apparent marginal cost and without conspicuously affecting or necessarily requiring permission from the external environment. Second, the introduction of library automation receives impetus from two directions: from professional librarians pressing for state-of-the-art technology and from the larger academic community, as it increasingly sees library automation related to information technology in general, and therefore inevitable. Third, revenue-generating activities in libraries, while not a new concept, have generally been limited in scope and are philosophically unacceptable to many librarians.

In prior research in Illinois schools, Richard L. Daft (1978) found support for the hypothesis that leader behavior would have greater influence on adoption of administrative or organizational innovations, whereas technical innovations would be more likely to be proposed and supported by professional employees. Similarly, Judith R. Blau and William McKinley (1979), studying innovation in architectural firms, introduced the concept of "work motifs" or ideas about work as determinants of innovation among professionals. They concluded that cognitive ideas and professional orientations were primary determinants of innovation. The relatively higher frequencies of changes in internal organization and automation found in this study and the lower frequencies of introduction of revenue-generating activities may be examples of these principles.

To delve further into the change phenomena, a change index was constructed to normalize all responses in terms of the time period for which the director was reporting. Thus, for a director who had been in a position for less than five years, the total number of reported changes was divided by the actual number of years in the position to arrive at an annual change rate. Since respondents were directed to report changes for no more than the past five years, for any director who had been in a position five years or more, the reported changes were divided by five to arrive at the annual change rate, or change index.

The average annual rate of change for all 42 libraries was 3.8. This is a noticeably lower rate than was reported by Helen A. Howard (1981) in her study of adoption of innovations by four academic libraries. In her study, the annual rates were 5.14, 7.14, 5.43, and 4.57, for an overall average of 6.3 innovations adopted annually. However, Howard's study asked libraries to identify "any changes which have made a noticeable difference to users and/or staff," an open-ended question that might be expected to elicit a different set of responses than the fixed list of possible changes in this study. The data, therefore, are not comparable. In addition, there is research which supports the hypothesis that adoption of innovation is positively correlated with organizational size, and all of the four libraries studied by Howard were medium to large in size.

CHANGE AND ORGANIZATION SIZE

Gerald Zaltman et al. (1973), J. Victor Baldridge and Robert Z. Burnham (1975), Michael K. Moch (1976), and Moch and

Edward V. Morse (1977) all reported that innovation was positively related to organizational size. Moch (1976) and Moch and Morse (1977) found, in studies of hospitals, that 32 percent of variance in adoption of innovation was accounted for by size alone. They also identified three intervening variables positively related to innovation: specialization, functional differentiation, and decentralization; however, the three intervening variables were defined as being functions of increased size of the organization.

In the Leader Activity Study, size was measured on the basis of the total university or college enrollment, as expressed in full-time equivalent (FTE) students. Institutions with enrollments greater than 30,000 FTE averaged 8.4 changes per year, whereas those with fewer than 10,000 students experienced an average of 4.07 changes per year. However, the pattern was not consistent for intermediate sizes, and in regression analysis, only a weak positive correlation was found between size and rates of change.

CHANGE AND LENGTH OF SERVICE OF THE DIRECTOR

A popular supposition, supported by the findings of M. W. Meyer (1975) and described in Chapter 2, is that a newly hired library director will implement a number of significant changes as soon as possible; a competing position states that the ability to make substantive change grows as the individual's experience and power in the organization develop over time. The scattergram in Figure 9.1 displays the index of change for each institution relative to the number of years the director has served in that position. A regression analysis was performed that shows a moderate negative association ($r = -.367$). In other words, the supposition that more change is made in the early years of a directorship is partially supported.

LEADER ACTIVITY AND CHANGE

Daft (1978), as previously described, found support for the hypothesis that leader behavior would influence adoption of

Figure 9.1
Change Rates and Director Years in Position

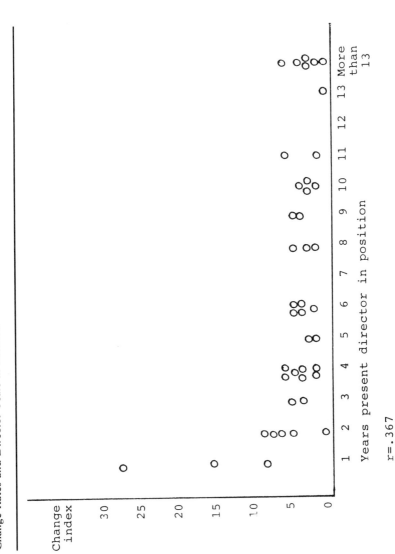

administrative or organizational innovations. The model described in Chapter 5 assumes that the managerial activities of the leader have significant impact on the entire organizational domain of the library, of which the introduction of change or adoption of innovation is one dimension. The principal objective of the study described in Chapter 6 was "to explore and describe relationships between the activities of library leaders . . . and their success in domain maintenance and growth." Research question 2 asks, "What interrelationships can be described between the managerial activities of the focal leader and the rate of organizational change in the library which he/she heads?"

The index of leader activity was created based on the total number of responses by the focal leader to the 40 activity questions, as described in Chapter 6. Responses 4 ("To a considerable extent") and 5 ("To an extreme extent") on the five-point scale were totaled for each respondent to create the leader activity index. In addition, for each of the six managerial roles a separate subset of the index was computed.

A regression analysis of the leader activity index by the change index was performed for the 42 respondents. Additional correlations were done between the leader activity index and each of the five categories of organizational change. The results are displayed in Table 9.1. Finally, leader activity subindexes for the six managerial roles were correlated with the five categories of organizational change, also displayed in Table 9.1.

Only two types of change are moderately positively associated with overall leader activity: changes in facilities and in the internal organization. There is also a slight positive association between overall leader activity and the introduction of revenue-generating programs and changes in relationships with other campus bodies. The association between leader activity and internal organizational changes is consistent with Daft's (1978) findings.

When each of the five categories of change is considered in relation to leader activity in the individual six managerial roles, slight to moderate associations are seen between activities in the Supervisor, Liaison, and Environment Monitor roles and the rate of changes in facilities, and between activities in the

Table 9.1
Organizational Change and Leader Activity (Values of *r*)

	Facilities	Automation	Categories of Change			Overall
			Revenue Activities	Relations w/campus	Internal Organization	
Leader Activity						
All roles	.34 *	.11	.21	.17	.31 *	.32 *
Supervisor	.34 *	-.13	.18	-.03	.06	
Liaison	.24	.00	.08	-.02	.13	
Environment monitor	.27	.02	.12	.05	.24	
Entrepreneur	-.11	.05	-.05	-.02	.20	
Spokesperson	.04	-.03	.09	-.07	.25	
Resource allocator	.10	-.18	.03	-.06	.12	

* p less than .20

Environment Monitor, Entrepreneur, and Spokesperson roles and the rate of changes in the internal organization. Other comparisons yield insignificant correlations.

These findings suggest that change as a whole is related to some degree to factors within the director's control but also significantly to factors within the environment such as economic conditions, political climate, and technological developments, which are outside the control of the individual director. In addition, the choice of activities for emphasis is likely to be more important than the overall level of activity. More generally, the ability of the director to influence and direct change may be the result of more complex and interrelated factors than this analysis covers.

Strategies for dealing with the external environment are somewhat different from specific managerial activities, although to a large extent they encompass specific activities. A strategy might be defined as a program or plan to develop a long-range relationship or position. The focal leaders were queried about their use of specific strategies in the Leader Activity Study, Part III. Simple numeric indexes of use of specific strategies were constructed on the basis of "yes" responses to the listed items for seven strategic responses to the environment:

- Altering the external environment's attitude toward the organization
- Influencing accepted norms regarding the organization
- Manipulating environmental demands on the organization
- Improving the organization's power position vis-à-vis the external environment
- Developing slack resources for use by the organization independently of the external environment
- Co-opting members of the external environment
- Developing cooperative arrangements with elements of the external environment

Weak positive correlations were found between higher rates of change and four of the seven strategies: altering the environment's attitudes, increasing the library's power base, developing slack resources, and co-optation of members of the external environment. On the other hand, there is negligible correlation with altering norms, manipulating demand, and developing cooperative arrangements. It is interesting to note that the latter three are traditional library strategies for dealing with the external environment, while the four strategies that correlate most strongly with organizational change are less so.

LEADER REPUTATIONAL EFFECTIVENESS AND CHANGE

The index of reputational effectiveness was derived from responses from the internal and external constituents to a 40-item questionnaire in which the items matched those of the leader activities. Responses of 4 ("Quite" effective) and 5 ("Extremely" effective) were tallied to create the index of reputational effectiveness. In a straightforward correlation of reputational effectiveness with the index of organizational changes of all types, only a negligible positive association was found. However, when individual change categories were analyzed, moderate positive associations were found between leader effectiveness ratings and (in rank order) changes in the internal library organization, facilities, and relationships with other campus entities.

Referring to the discussion of findings regarding the association of leader activity in the six managerial roles, one finds that role activity was also slightly to moderately positively associated with changes in facilities and internal organization. Unanswered is the question of which variable, if any, precedes which. While it is tempting to assume that activity leads to change, which in turn leads to reputational effectiveness, there is some evidence in the research of Tsui and Karwan (1984) to the effect that reputational effectiveness precedes organizational success, rather than the reverse.

10

Key Leadership Types

We are unable to define [leadership], but we sure seem to know it when we see it.

(Mintzberg, 1982)

Leader activity, reputational effectiveness, and management of domain or change formed the three principal dimensions used to describe academic library directors. Combining individual scores for all three dimensions yields a richer perspective on the leader's role than does the study of single or paired dimensions. All possible combinations of the three dimensions result in the eight leader types arrayed in Figure 10.1. In brief, the eight types have the following characteristics:

Type I:
  High reputational effectiveness
  High organizational change
  High leader activity

Type II:
  High reputational effectiveness
  High organizational change
  Low leader activity

Figure 10.1
Eight Leadership Types

Dimension	Leadership Type							
	I	II	III	IV	V	VI	VII	VIII
Reputational effectiveness	High N=29				Low N=13			
Organizational change	High N=9		Low N=20		High N=3		Low N=10	
Leader activity	High N=6 Energizer	Low N=3	High N=9 Sustainer	Low N=11 Politiciar.	High N=1	Low N=2	High N=3	Low N=7 Retiree
Code	HHH	HHL	HLH	HLL	LHH	LHL	LLH	LLL
Type	I	II	III	IV	V	VI	Vii	VIII

N=42

Type III:
  High reputational effectiveness
  Low organizational change
  High leader activity

Type IV:
  High reputational effectiveness
  Low organizational change
  Low leader activity

Type V:
  Low reputational effectiveness
  High organizational change
  High leader activity

Type VI:
  Low reputational effectiveness
  High organizational change
  Low leader activity

Type VII:
  Low reputational effectiveness
  Low organizational change
  High leader activity

Type VIII:
  Low reputational effectiveness
  Low organizational change
  Low leader activity

For economy of language, in further discussion two conventions are observed in referring to the eight types. They are referenced either as Type I, and so on, or as HHH (High reputational effectiveness, High organizational change, High leader activity), HLL (High reputational effectiveness, Low organizational change, Low leader activity), and so forth. A more detailed discussion of the criteria utilized to determine high and low ranking and tests of significance is found in Appendix B.

FOUR KEY TYPES

Four leader types occur with greater frequency than would be expected by chance: Type I (HHH), Type III (HLH), Type IV (HLL), and Type VIII (LLL). These four dominant types are considered in detail.

Each of the four is given a descriptive sobriquet to more readily distinguish it from the others. Type I (HHH) may be called "the Energizer," based on the high levels of activity, change, and reputation enjoyed. Type III (HLH), "the Sustainer," enjoys a high reputation, is highly active, but heads a library experiencing relatively little organizational change. Type IV (HLL), in spite of low leader activity and low organizational change, is also reputationally effective and may be termed "the Politician." Finally, Type VIII (LLL) might best be called "the Retiree," as it appears that this director is relatively inactive as a leader, heads a fairly unchanging organization, and is not highly regarded—or perhaps is simply disregarded—by colleagues.

The four key types were compared on each of the three principal dimensions—leader activity, reputational effectiveness, and organizational change—as well as on use of environmental influence strategies, professional involvement, university activities, and career patterns. The comparisons encompassed not only the four types under examination here but comparison with the mean scores for the entire study population.

MANAGERIAL ROLE ACTIVITY

When the leader activity scores for the key types are compared to each other and to the entire population of leaders, certain differences become apparent. The Energizer scores significantly higher in activities in the Supervisor, Spokesperson, and Entrepreneur roles than the overall population and also scores higher on the mean for overall activity, as represented by the sum of all activity items.

The Sustainer also scores significantly high in the Supervisor role; the only other noticeably high role is the Liaison role, although again, the Sustainer scores high on overall activity. The Politician, on the other hand, scores significantly below the mean for the Supervisor, Liaison, and Spokesperson roles. Although the Politician scores below the mean for the other roles and for overall activity, these scores are not statistically significant.

Finally, the Retiree scores below the population mean for every role and for overall activity. However, the only significant low role score is for the Liaison role. Since by definition the Energizer and the Sustainer are higher than the mean in total leader activity, it is not surprising that their scores are significantly higher than the mean. However, although the Politician and the Retiree are expected to be below the population mean and this is the case, their scores are not significantly lower.

Within a single leader type, differences in allocation of activity are noted. The Energizer shows the highest overall activity level of the four types, but none of the individual role activities within the type vary significantly from the overall activity level for the Energizer. The same is true for the Sustainer, whose overall activity level is only marginally lower than that of the Energizer. On the other hand, the Politician's activities as Supervisor (an internally focused role) are significantly lower than this type's activity mean, and as Entrepreneur (an externally focused role) are significantly higher than for the activity mean for the Politician. In the same vein, the activity levels of the Retiree in the Supervisor (internal) and Liaison (external) roles are both well below the Retiree's activity mean.

ENVIRONMENTAL INFLUENCE STRATEGIES

Again, environmental influence strategies are an extension of leader activity of a somewhat more purposeful sort. Only one significant instance is apparent, wherein the Politician type makes significantly less use of the strategy of attempting to influence norms which the environment applies to the organization than is made of other strategies. As noted in Chapter 8, the overall utilization of influence strategies is high (.77 out of 1.0) throughout the study population, and little difference is noted among strategies or among roles, as noted here.

ORGANIZATIONAL CHANGE

It is to be expected that the Energizer will display significantly higher change categories, since by definition Type I is above the population mean in overall change. In the same way, low-change categories are to be expected for the remaining three key types. These suppositions are only partially supported. The Energizer's change level is significantly higher than the population mean for all five categories of change, the Retiree's level lower for all categories. However, the Sustainer is significantly lower in three change categories—automation, campus relationships, and internal organization—and is close to the mean in the facilities category. The Politician ranks significantly lower in four of the five change categories, while in the fifth, Politicians exceed their own means for all categories of change.

REPUTATIONAL EFFECTIVENESS

Three of the four key types (I, III, and IV) are by definition higher than the population mean in reputational effectiveness; Type VIII is by definition below the mean. However, the mean scores for the three high-reputation types are all either precisely at or extremely close to the mean for all high-reputation cases. This is explained by simple examination of the data, which reveal that the three high-reputation individuals who fall into Type II (HHL) and are excluded from the four key types are among the four highest-reputation cases, whereas the remaining high-reputation cases are fairly evenly distributed within the entire range of high-reputation scores. As expected, the mean normalized reputation score for Type VIII is well below the population mean; however, it is close to the mean for the low-reputation group.

PROFESSIONAL INVOLVEMENT

The Energizer type shows the lowest mean professional involvement index of the four key types. This score reflects lower-than-average activity in all four of the grouped categories, which is especially noticeable in journals read or scanned and conferences attended. The Retiree shows an unusually high number of workshops and courses attended, while the Sustainer is significantly low in the same category. Overall, the Retiree has the highest average professional involvement index, although not significantly above the population mean.

UNIVERSITY COMMITTEES

University committee participation is close to the population mean or somewhat higher for the Energizer and the Politician, and significantly lower for the Sustainer and the Retiree.

CAREER PATTERNS

The Energizer type had the youngest mean age, 45.33 years, and the highest proportion of women; this is to be expected, since the women tended to be younger than the men in the study, with a mean age of 45.7 versus 49.25 for the men. The Retirees' mean age was the highest, at 51.29 years versus a population mean of 48.4 years. The three high-reputation groups all were younger than the population mean.

Again, Energizers tended to have occupied their positions for the shortest time, 3.5 years versus a population mean of 7.5 years, while Retirees had a mean tenure in position of 11.86 years. The Retirees had worked in the largest number of libraries, 4.71 on average, perhaps reflecting their greater age, whereas Politicians had worked in the fewest, 2.91 on average. Finally, the total number of positions occupied for all four types was close to the population mean, although highest at 5.33 for the Energizer and slightly below the mean for the other three types.

Educationally, the greatest proportion of doctorates were held by Retirees, fully 57 percent of whom held some form of doctorate. Fifty percent of Energizers held doctorates, above the population mean of 40 percent, while 33 percent of Sustainers and 27 percent of Politicians held doctorates. When holders of any advanced degree above the M.L.S. are combined, however, differences are less beteween types. Sixty-seven percent of Energizers, 66 percent of Sustainers, 63 percent of Politicians, and 71 percent of Retirees hold advanced degrees, as compared to 64 percent of the total population.

PROFILE: THE ENERGIZER

Turning to the individual types, it is possible to sketch a profile for each, based on characteristics in which it resembles or differs from the other key types or from the study population means. Obviously, the description of a type is drawn from averages and may not describe any specific individual.

The Energizer, who ranks above the population mean on all three principal dimensions—reputational effectiveness, leader activity, and organizational change—might be characterized as the leader of what D. E. Berlew (1977) termed an "excited" organization. The excited organization is led by an individual who exercises a great deal of personal influence, and it experiences a high rate of innovation.

The Energizer enjoys a high reputation, although only minutely higher than the mean for all high reputation leaders in this study. Leader activity is high by definition, .81 (on a scale of 0.0 to 1.0) as compared to a population mean of .56. In terms of the extent of specific activities, the Energizer focuses relatively more attention on the Spokesperson (an externally focused role), Entrepreneur (internal focus), and Resource Allocator (internal and external) roles than on other roles. In addition, Supervisor (internal) activity is signficantly higher than for the population as a whole. Thus, this type is seen as focusing activity both internally and externally, with somewhat greater emphasis on the internal organization.

The Energizer's library is experiencing the highest rate of change of any of the four key types. Among the five categories of change, the greatest proportion of changes is in the internal organization of the library. However, all other types of change are also high, with facilities changes being the lowest. Since the Energizer has been in position the shortest time of any key type, only 3.5 years, which is little more than one-half the time of the next shortest-tenure type, it may be that these emphases reflect the relative quickness with which internal organization change can take place and the long-term nature of planning and financing facilities changes, particularly building construction and remodeling. The types of change are also consistent with the relatively greater emphasis on leader activities focused on the internal organization.

The career pattern of the Energizer suggests youth, energy, and rapid career development. The Energizer group includes both males and females who are younger than their colleagues in the study by an average of six years, have occupied the greatest number of professional positions (5.33), and have worked in the second greatest number of libraries (4.17). Fifty percent of them hold doctorates, and 67 percent hold an advanced degree of some kind in addition to the M.L.S.

Professionally, Energizers read or scan fewer professional journals and attend fewer conferences and workshops than do their colleagues. Overall, their professional involvement, as represented by the Professional Involvement Index, is nearly 25 percent lower than the population mean. Again, this finding is consistent with the emphasis in focus on the library rather than the environment external to the library. However, given that Energizers have served on 6.33 university committees in the prior three years, compared to 6.07 for the general population, it would appear that external focus is selectively directed closer to the environment most directly affecting the library.

The Energizer thus emerges as a leader who focuses on the organization and management of the library, turning attention to outside arenas principally where they are seen as having immediate impact on the library. The result is a rapidly changing library and high esteem for the leader. The Energizer's motto might be: A dynamic, well-run library is its own best advertisement!

PROFILE: THE SUSTAINER

The Sustainer ranks above the mean in reputational effectiveness and in leader activity but heads a relatively low-change library. Reputationally, the Sustainer ranks precisely on the mean for the high reputation group. Sustainers are by definition high-activity leaders and do not differ from Energizers in overall activity. They expend proportionately more effort as Liaison (external focus), Entrepreneur (internal), and Resource Allocator (internal and external). Additionally, they have the highest Supervisor (internal) score of any of the key types, at .62. Thus, Sustainers, who are high in all leader activity roles, focus fairly evenly internally and externally.

Change in libraries headed by Sustainers is by definition lower than average. Within this framework, Sustainer libraries experienced significantly less change in automation, in relationships with other campus entities, and in the internal library organization than did the population as a whole. Among Sustainer libraries, relatively greater facilities changes had taken place than any other category. Since changes were limited to those which had taken place in the prior five years, and the typical Sustainer had been in position 8.33 years, these findings may exclude changes in relationships with other campus entities and internal organizational changes that might have taken place during the early years of the Sustainer's occupancy of the directorship. These changes in organizational structure and relationships can be made relatively swiftly and at low apparent marginal cost. On the other hand, achieving facilities changes is a long-term process, which would result in relatively more of those being evident in Sustainer libraries. The markedly low rate of introduction of automation does not readily lend itself to explanation on this basis, however.

The Sustainer library, in Berlew's taxonomy, would then be characterized as a "neutral" or "satisfied" organization, experiencing relatively little change but stable and efficient under competent and comfortable leadership.

The career patterns of Sustainers show individuals who are marginally younger (47.0 years) than the mean and primarily male (89 percent). They have occupied their positions for an average of 8.33 years, close to the population mean, but have worked in slightly fewer libraries (3.44) and occupied slightly fewer professional positions (4.89). Educationally, 33 percent of them hold doctorates, below the average, but when advanced degrees beyond the M.L.S. are combined, 67 percent hold such degrees, slightly above the average.

Sustainers rank below the population mean on the Professional Involvement Index, although above Energizers. Sustainers present few papers or panel programs and attend few workshops, but their rates of participation in other professional association activities, attendence at conferences, and professional reading are typical of the study population.

University committee participation by Sustainers is significantly low. Since Sustainers are held in high esteem, one inference might be that the Sustainer library is highly regarded but is viewed by both the leader and the university as somewhat removed from university affairs.

The profile of the Sustainer that emerges is of an active director of a contented and stable library, an individual who is in few ways atypical of directors as a group, one who balances attention between the library and its environment but is not heavily involved in the running of the university. The Sustainer's motto might be: Competency is also comfort; steady as she goes!

PROFILE: THE POLITICIAN

The Politician demonstrates low leader activity and heads a low-change library yet receives high effectiveness ratings by constituents. Furthermore, Politicians make up 26 percent of the study population and one-third of the members of the four key types. The size of this group contradicts the assumption that high activity level results in high effectiveness ratings.

Reputationally, Politicians resemble Energizers and Sustainers in being extremely close to the mean score for the high reputation group. Their total activity level is the lowest of the four key types, at .40, well below the population mean of .56. Among leader activity roles, they expend little effort on Supervisor (internal focus) activities and a great deal on Entrepreneur activities (internal). Compared to other types and to the population, Politicians rank significantly low in Supervisor, Liaison (external), and Spokesperson (external) roles. Entrepreneur activity items all have to do with initiating, planning, and implementing changes in the library. However, the Politician by definition heads a relatively low-change library.

Within categories of organizational change, the Politician's library experiences greatest change in the area of automation, and second greatest in internal library organization. Politicians' libraries are significantly below the population means in every category but automation. Of the four key types, only the Energizer has a higher rate of automation. One might speculate that automation is a desired innovation with high visibility that affects reputation. However, examination of the data for the three cases that fall into the low-reputation and high-change types (Types V and VI) shows that the mean automation score for this limited number of cases is .24, more than twice as high as the mean automation score for Politicians. Because of the tiny number of cases of high automation/low reputation, care must be taken in drawing conclusions, however.

Politicians' career patterns resemble those of Sustainers. Their average age is 47.0, and 82 percent are men. They have occupied their present positions for somewhat less time, 6.91 years, and have worked in fewer libraries, 2.91 on average. Educationally, they have the smallest proportion of doctorates of the four key types, 27 percent, and the largest proportion of second master's degrees, 36 percent.

The Professional Involvement Index for Politicians is slightly below the population mean and similar to that for Sustainers. Politicians read and scan fewer professional journals than do Sustainers, Retirees, and the total study population. Their attendance at conferences is close to the mean. Participation in professional association activity is above the mean, and the highest for the four key types. While papers published and panels presented is close to the population mean, it is considerably higher than the same category of activity by Sustainers.

Politicians have the highest level of participation on university committees, 7.27, of any of the four key types and are above the population mean of 6.07. This is particularly interesting in light of findings by Pfeffer and Salancik (1974) and Pfeffer and Moore (1980) that academic department membership on important university committees was positively related to budget allocations. (However, Hills and Mahoney [1978], in a similar study, were unable to replicate this finding.)

The Politician is something of a puzzle. In many respects this type resembles the Sustainer, and the Politician's library would also be characterized in Berlew's terms as "neutral" or "satisfied." The few respects in which politicians differ from Sustainers have to do with the nature of organizational change, the relatively lower levels of leader activity, somewhat faster career path, and higher involvement in professional activities (exclusive of reading/scanning journals) and in university committees. The characteristic which thus emerges as distinctive is visibility, in terms of the choice of a highly visible category of change, association activities that bring visibility, and active involvement in university governance.

The profile of the Politician is of a library director who is highly selective about the choice of what activities to engage in and what library programs to implement. The high reputation enjoyed is likely to come in part from the stability and effectiveness of the library and in part from the director's visible role as a professional and university leader. Motto: Visibility is important; maintain a high profile!

PROFILE: THE RETIREE

Type VIII includes 17 percent of the study population. Individuals of the Retiree type engage in limited leader activity, experience little organizational change, and are held in relatively low esteem by their colleagues. As a group they are older than their peers, with a mean age of 51.29. Men and women are represented in about the same proportions as in the study as a whole. Retirees have the longest tenure in position of the key types, 11.86 years. They have worked in somewhat more than the average number of libraries but have occupied somewhat fewer total positions. Their educational level is higher than the other key types and than the study population. Fifty-seven percent hold doctorates, and 71 percent hold any advanced degree above the M.L.S.

Reputationally, Retirees rank slightly below the mean score for all low-reputation directors. Without exception, leader activity scores for all roles are below the population mean. In terms of the Retiree's own allocation of role activity, proportionately greater effort is expended on the Resource Allocator role and less on the Supervisor and Liaison roles. However, the Retiree's overall activity score is a little greater than is the Politician's.

Organizational change in Retirees' libraries is significantly lower than the population mean in all categories, and there is little distinction among categories. Retirees read and scan professional journals at a rate about the population mean but well above the Energizer and the Politician. They attend conferences at about the mean but participate in workshops and courses at the highest level of any of the key types and at a rate significantly above the population mean. It was noted in Chapter 7, however, that workshop and course attendance showed a moderate negative association with reputational effectiveness. Retirees' association activity is higher than the mean, and higher than any key type except the Politician. However, they deliver and publish papers and panels at a rate lower than the mean and lower than any key type except the Sustainer. Taken as a whole, the Retiree's Professional Involvement Index is the highest of the four key types. Counting association activity and publications and presentations as active involvement and the remaining four categories as passive involvement, it appears that this high index score is primarily attributable to a greater number of passive activities. Retirees' relatively high level of activity away from the university could be interpreted as an indication that the library director has little direct involvement in the library and the university and seeks professional stimulation and satisfaction elsewhere. It might also be an indication that the Retiree feels inadequate as a director and attends professional meetings and continuing education activities in an effort to gather insights and information that will bring him/her back into the mainstream. Since professional currency is one of the principal purposes of conferences and workshops, this behavior is a logical response.

University committee assignments do not reflect the elder statesman status that might be expected to come with longevity as library director. At 3.86 committee assignments, Retirees score significantly below the mean, although not as low as Sustainers.

The profile that emerges for the Retiree is one of passivity. The Retiree does not enjoy the high reputation of the more visible Politician or the active involvement in the running of the library that the Sustainer does. The library headed by a Retiree would best fit Berlew's concept of the dissatisfied and decaying organization. The Retiree's motto: Continuity is a virtue. It's best not to rock the boat.

PROFILE SUMMARY

Intuitively, the Energizer type is an appealing one that leads to organizational excitement and to high innovation. However, the literature of innovation points out that innovation is a cyclical phenomenon (Zaltman et al., 1973; Daft, 1978) and that periods of high innovation are followed by periods of sustained implementation and consolidation. Robert D. Dewar and Robert B. Duncan (1977) proposed that alternating or cyclical sets of organizational behaviors are appropriate for the stages of innovation and implementation. Thus, low-change Sustainers and Politicians have an appropriate role in the organizational life cycle.

Of the four groups, the Politician is the most frequent (26 percent), then the Sustainer (21 percent), followed by the Retiree (17 percent), and the least frequent of the four modal types, the Energizer (14 percent). These four key types represent 78.5 percent of the study population but only half of the eight possible types. Understanding would be enriched if it had been possible to analyze, for example, high change/low reputation leaders, or those who show high activity but low reputation, and to compare them with their high reputation parallels.

11

Implications and Practical Applications

How can an understanding of differing styles of leadership among academic library directors be put to practical use to improve the functioning of our libraries? More effective library leadership will not come about unless university administrators and decision makers, library educators, library staff, and library administrators thoroughly understand the purpose of leadership and how it is carried out.

Every player in this cast of characters must not only understand but also expect performance based on the symbolic and agenda-setting roles of the leader. They must comprehend the difference between leadership and management and the extent to which both are required of the university library director and other library administrators. They must be fully aware of where the university and its library system are in the organizational life cycle and must take that into account in their expectations for change. Above all, they must act on the knowledge that while different leadership styles and behaviors are appropriate to different organizational circumstances, the underlying role of the leader in creating and affirming the shared vision that motivates the library remains the same.

Although the Leader Activity Study focused exclusively on the academic library director and this discussion refers to the same position, it should be noted that each library administrator and manager, from the department head level upward, fulfills leadership roles and in each case occupies the critical nexus between an internal operating organization (the department, division, or section) and an external environment (the other library units and the environment outside the library). Thus, the implications for the director apply to all library managers.

The underlying themes apply to each of the four constituencies in differing ways.

UNIVERSITY ADMINISTRATORS AND FACULTY

Those who search for, hire, and evaluate the library chief executive bear a special responsibility. Nowhere is the personnel truism that the hiring decision is the most important decision an organization makes clearer than here. It is apparent from scanning advertisements and job descriptions that the quest for effective leadership is on, yet increasingly those announcements are laundry lists of an impossible array of expertise in every aspect of library operations, as if what was lacking in the past was knowledge of specific applications.

Before an effective search for a library leader at any level, top or middle management, can be conducted, the university must consider several critical questions:

- First, how does the list of desired abilities and credentials relate to the stated mission and goals of the library?
- Is the university consciously or unconsciously seeking a leader who will resolve the "library problem" and remove it from further administrative attention?
- Has the library's recent experience been one of relative stability or of tumultuous change, or somewhere in between?
- How successful has past change been in terms of ease of implementation and in terms of the desired results?
- Do the desired abilities and qualifications match the library's place in its organizational life cycle?
- What is the university administration willing to do to assist the library chief executive in being a successful leader, in terms of both resources and authority?

- Do all players understand and accept the dual inside-outside role of the library director?
- Does the position description focus on technical skills or on more generalizable skills such as interpersonal communication, planning, negotiating, coalition building, and decision making?

Search committees typically are "rainbow" bodies representing a spectrum of special interests. The less successful the library has been in the past in fulfilling its mission, the more likely that each constituency—faculty, students, library staff, administrators outside the library—will have a unique agenda. By considering questions such as those above, the committee may be able to transcend diverse individual wants and expectations and focus on the overall effectiveness of the library and the role of the leader in guiding it.

Once a shared understanding is reached regarding the required balance among the various leadership roles, questions asked of professional references, screening criteria, and the nature of the interview process will need to be tailored accordingly. It is vital that every step of the recruitment process by guided by the same set of assumptions and expectations.

THE LIBRARY STAFF

The expectations of library staff for the director are often wildly unrealistic. Their hope is, simply, that the director will be all things to all people.

The director is expected to pay close attention to each staff member and to each library operating unit, all the while busily promoting the library's interests outside the library. The director will, of course, inspire and guide planned change that will keep the library in, if not the forefront, at least the mainstream of current library practice, but while doing so will be mindful of staff opinions and wishes and will prevent changes that upset routine, result in extensive staff shifts, or appear to focus on one aspect of library operations at the expense of another. The director is expected to lead and to take responsibility for decisions but not to violate group norms, the organizational culture that may well have preceded the director and may be expected to endure after she or he has departed.

These often contradictory expectations are not unique to library staff but mirror the broad catchall of individual and organizational agendas that are brought to the library director's doorstep by other constituencies as well. Furthermore, the polymorphous director actually *is* what is required, to a significant degree, and the wise director will attempt to address, if not to satisfy, all agendas. If staff are more aware of the multiple roles which the leader must play, however, they will better be able to understand and accept why one activity takes precedence over another, how priorities are set, how negotiations and compromise are an essential part of decision making. The leader can play an important part in educating staff by articulating how she or he sees the directorial role and the means for carrying out that role.

LIBRARY EDUCATORS

Without a doubt, it is impossible adequately to train library managers in entry-level M.L.S. programs. Whether it is possible formally to train leaders at all is also open to question. Nevertheless, library education can approach the leadership problem on two levels, developing an understanding of the theory and practice of leadership and contributing to the overall socialization of students into a profession that puts a high premium on effective leadership.

At least one model of leadership studies has been implemented, albeit for undergraduate students, at the College of Wooster in Ohio. In an interdisciplinary program, students explore the theoretical and practical aspects of leadership, using as resources such diverse texts as Plato's *The Republic*, Machiavelli's *The Prince*, and biographies of Chrysler chairman Lee Iacocca and Martin Luther King, Jr. Their studies also include discussions with government officials, corporate executives, and leaders in higher education (Watkins, 1986). The stated purpose is to give students an acquaintance with the concept of leadership as a legitimate area of intellectual inquiry, rather than to attempt to teach leadership.

Library schools have long taught introductory management courses to M.L.S. students. There, too, the objective is not to train practicing managers but to give an acquaintance with the essential concepts that not only form the foundations upon which future management skills may be developed but also round out the student's understanding of the organizational environment within which even the most junior librarian must function. Inclusion of units of study regarding leadership is a logical extension of management courses; within the framework of this research, it becomes an essential element in completing the paradigm of what effective leaders and managers do.

Socialization of apprentices into the culture and norms of a profession is a process that takes place during education for the profession and during one's early work experience. Discussions of leadership in general and library leadership in particular, as well as meetings with acknowledged leaders, during library school is an essential starting point for the profession.

Entry-level librarians armed with a general awareness, if not understanding, of the multiple roles and political aspects of leadership will be significantly better prepared to be followers and subordinates, to learn by example and from mentors, and to ultimately mature into leaders themselves.

THE ROLE OF PROFESSIONAL ASSOCIATIONS

The problems of effective leadership are not unique to higher education or to academic libraries. While scholarly studies of leadership have not led in anything approaching a straight line toward a leadership paradigm for today's organizations, a number of organizations have undertaken to bring concentrated focus on the problem.

The Center for Creative Leadership in Greensboro, North Carolina,[1] conducts studies and publishes reports, audiotapes, and a newsletter (*Issues and Observations*) on a broad spectrum of leadership concerns. Topics range from a review of management evaluation instruments to audiotapes on creative leadership to consideration of assessment centers for leadership appraisal.

The Leadership Studies Program of the Independent Sector, based in Washington, D.C., is directed by former Secretary of Health, Education, and Welfare John W. Gardner.[2] *The Tasks of Leadership*, authored by Gardner (1986), is a particularly succinct summary of the symbolic and meaning-creating aspects of leadership.

Southern Illinois University has sponsored a series of leadership symposia that have been published under a variety of titles by the Southern Illinois University Press.

The American Association for Higher Education has in preparation, with the participation of a representative from the Associaton of College and Research Libraries, a monograph dealing with conducting an effective search for nonfaculty administrative positions in higher education.

A paradigm shift—in this case, from leader as manager to leader as articulator of meaning—does not take place easily or quickly. In recent years a good deal of attention at library conferences has been paid to effective management, for all levels of managers, dealing with nearly every conceivable managerial technique and concern. Program organizers could do much to bring about discussion and debate on what constitutes effective library leadership, who exercises it and how.

THE LIBRARY DIRECTOR

What of the library director, the focus of the study? When Arthur M. McAnally and Robert B. Downs published the results of their survey of directors who had recently left their posts in academic libraries in 1973, they were able to point to an underlying assumption that the directorship was an earned sinecure, a reward for good and faithful service. In today's tumultuous times the director is expected to have a direct and dynamic impact on the library, on its services and organization, and on the way it adapts to changed circumstances. And without doubt change is the order of the day, although not at all times in all libraries.

How, then, must directors, present and aspiring, adjust their attitudes and behaviors to succeed? In general terms they must:

- Understand the meaning-creating role of the library director
- Learn to focus energy and activities both toward internal library operations and staff and toward the university as a whole
- Recognize that different stages in the organization's life cycle will require different emphases
- Accept the idea that the same person may not be the appropriate leader for all organizational circumstances
- Utilize the dual concept of management and leadership as essential and related functions each of which requires different activities and focuses
- Learn methods of formulating goals and objectives for the library and consciously communicate this vision to the library and the university, frequently and consistently.

A library director who can do this understands the assigned role both as an administrator and as a leader.

NOTES

1. Center for Creative Leadership, P.O. Box p-1, Greensboro, NC 27402-1660.

2. Leadership Studies Program, Independent Sector, 1828 L Street N.W., Washington, D.C. 20036.

APPENDIX A1

Leader Activity Study Questionnaire, Library Directors

LEADER ACTIVITY STUDY

March 1985

Return completed questionnaire to:

Leader Activity Study
489 Lagunaria Lane
Alameda, CA 94501

PART I

These statements refer to activities a manager might or might not perform. You are asked to indicate the extent to which you, as library chief executive on your campus, actually perform or carry out each of these activities.

In answering, use the following scale and place the appropriate number in the blank space to the left of each statement.

PERFORMANCE OF ACTIVITY<

1	2	3	4	5
Not at all	To a small extent	To a moderate extent	To a considerable extent	To an extreme extent

PERFORMANCE
OF ACTIVITY

Example:

1. Running departmental meetings.

_4_

BE SURE to answer every item. Do not skip any.

112

1. Evaluating subordinate job performance.

2. Initiating new ideas for services and/or operations.

3. Planning and implementing changes in the library.

4. Distributing budgeted resources.

5. Integrating subordinates' goals (e.g. career goals and work preferences) with the university's and library's goals and objectives.

6. Forwarding important information to subordinates.

7. Attending university social functions to keep up contacts.

8. Keeping up with professional trends and changes that might have an impact on the library.

9. Serving as an expert or providing advice to people outside of the library.

10. Initiating controlled change in the library.

11. Making decisions about time parameters for upcoming programs.

12. Directing the work of subordinates.

13. Allocating human resources to specific jobs or tasks.

14. Attending conferences or meetings of other groups or organizations.

Appendix A1 (*Continued*)

_____ 15. Keeping up with information on the progress of programs and operations throughout the university.

_____ 16. Keeping others informed of the library's future plans.

_____ 17. Solving problems by instituting needed changes in the library.

_____ 18. Preventing the loss or threat of loss of human or capital resources valued by the library.

_____ 19. Resolving conflicts between subordinates.

_____ 20. Keeping track of subordinates' training and special skills as they relate to job assignments--so as to facilitate their personal growth and development.

_____ 21. Attending social functions as a representative of the library.

_____ 22. Keeping up with technological developments related to the library and the university.

_____ 23. Answering letters or inquiries on behalf of the library.

_____ 24. Allocating monies within the library.

_____ 25. Giving negative feedback by criticizing subordinates' actions when appropriate.

_____ 26. Scanning the external environment for new opportunities to improve services or operations.

_____ 27. Serving on committees and/or task forces as a representative of the library.

...roviding other people with information about the library's activities and plans.

29. Deciding which programs to provide resources to (human resources, materials, dollars, equipment, etc.)

30. Seeing to it that subordinates are alert to problems that need attention.

31. Staying attuned to the informal communication networks of the university.

32. Gathering information about library users, other units of the university, new professional developments.

33. Allocating equipment or materials.

34. Using your authority to insure that subordinates accomplish important tasks.

35. Touring facilities or work stations for observational purposes.

36. Developing contacts with important people outside the library.

37. Learning about new ideas originating outside the library.

38. Providing new employees with adequate training for and introduction to the job at hand.

39. Reading reports on activities and plans of other units of the university.

40. Obtaining adequate resources to administer library service programs and build library collections.

Appendix A1 (*Continued*)

PART II

For each of the organizational changes listed below, please indicate by circling Y (yes) or N (no) whether this change has taken place in your library during the past five years or since your appointment, whichever is the shorter time period.

1. Facilities changes:

Y N   1.1 Introduction of open stack compact shelving

Y N   1.2 Introduction of closed stack compact shelving

Y N   1.3 Introduction of remote storage for part of the collections

Y N   1.4 Conversion of periodical backfiles to microform

Y N   1.5 Approval for planning new building, addition or renovation

Y N   1.6 Construction of new building, addition or renovation

Y N   1.7 Other (Please describe) _____

_____

2. Introduction of major automation:

Y N   2.1 Automated circulation

Y N   2.2 Online public catalog

Y   N   2.3 Automated acquisitions

Y   N   2.4 Online cataloging system

Y   N   2.5 Online serials control

Y   N   2.6 Automated document delivery system

Y   N   2.7 Other (Please describe) _____

3.   Introduction of revenue-generating activities in the library:

Y   N   3.1 Online bibliographic search services for profit

Y   N   3.2 Copying services generating income

Y   N   3.3 Sales of student supplies: pencils, paper, etc.

Y   N   3.4 Sales of library publications

Y   N   3.5 Sales of discarded books

Y   N   3.6 Customized reference and delivery services

Y   N   3.7 Public programs or workshops for fee

Y   N   3.8 Other (Please describe) _____
                                     _____

Appendix A1 (*Continued*)

4. Changes in relationships with other campus entities:

Y N   4.1 Developing personnel office separate from central university office

Y N   4.2 Development of separate personnel policies and procedures

Y N   4.3 Development of computing services office separate from central university service

Y N   4.4 Introduction of system of billing faculty for overdue or lost books

Y N   4.5 Major change in method of allocating book and periodical funds

Y N   4.6 Other (Please describe) _____

5. Organizational changes:

Y N   5.1 Shifting from salaried personnel to contract services for any aspect of library operations
        5.11 Please list contract services introduced _____

Y N   5.2 Reorganization of entire library system

Y N 5.3 Reorganization of a major division

Y N 5.4 Creation of a new upper level management position

Y N 5.5 Creation of a new department or division

Y N 5.6 Closing one or more branch libraries

Y N 5.7 Opening one or more branch libraries

Y N 5.8 Development of non-print collections and services

Y N 5.9 Development of computer software collections

Y N 5.10 Introduction of computer labs into library

Y N 5.11 Other (Please describe) _____

_____

6. Other major library changes:

Appendix A1 (*Continued*)

PART III

The following list includes a variety of possible methods which a library director might make use of in seeking support for changes in library programs or for maintaining adequate budget allocations. For each, please consider whether it is an activity in which you, or your library on your behalf, regularly engage. The term "University decision makers" is used to refer to any individual or formal group which makes decisions regarding allocation of resources or approves library policy matters, library operations changes, facilities changes, and the like. Circle Y (yes) or N (no) for each activity.

Y   N   1.   Written budget justification, annually or more frequently.

Y   N   2.   Seeking support of the academic senate for changes in library programs.

Y   N   3.   Cooperative projects between the library and other libraries outside the university.

Y   N   4.   Working with professional organizations to alter standards.

Y   N   5.   Creating revenue-producing activities in and for the library.

Y   N   6.   Distribution of library annual reports to university decision makers.

Y   N   7.   Seeking support of community groups outside the university for library activities.

Y   N   8.   Lobbying legislators directly for changes in budget allocations.

Y N 9. Cooperative projects between the library and other campus
            support units, such as the computer center.

Y N 10. Oral budget justification, annually or more frequently.

Y N 11. Public relations programs directed toward the campus in
            general.

Y N 12. Your own membership on university decision making bodies.

Y N 13. Seeking support of student organizations for changes in
            library programs.

Y N 14. Obtaining grant or private donor funding for new library
            programs.

Y N 15. Personal interactions with university decision makers.

Y N 16. Public relations programs directed toward specific segments
            of the campus community.

Y N 17. Establishing cost-recovery services in the library.

Y N 18. Invoking published standards in budget or programmatic
            proposals.

Y N 19. Seeking support of the Friends of the Library for library
            activities.

Y N 20. Special library services to influential university individuals
            or groups.

121

Appendix A1 (*Continued*)

Y N 21. Sponsorship of social events to which university decision makers are present.

Y N 22. Use of members of the university community outside the library on library task forces and committees.

Y N 23. Working with state or system bodies to alter budget formulas or standards.

Y N 24. Membership of other library staff on university decision making bodies.

Y N 25. Cooperative projects between the library and schools or colleges of the university.

Y N 26. Attendance at social events where university decision makers are present.

Y N 27. Seeking support of the faculty library committee for changes in library programs.

PART IV

These questions concerning your personal and organizational background will provide useful information for the study. Please answer all of them. All information will be held confidential and the respondent will not be individually identified in any way.

1. How many years have you been in your present position? Round to the nearest whole year.

------Years

2. How many different positions have you held as a library professional?

------Positions

3. How many separate libraries or library systems have you worked in?

------Libraries

4. How old were you on your last birthday?

------years

5. What is your sex?

------Female (5.1)   ------Male (5.2)

123

Appendix A1 (*Continued*)

6. What is your level of graduate education? Please indicate the category which most nearly describes you.

```
_____MLS/BLS (6.1)
_____MLS plus other master's degree. Subject_____(6.2)
_____MLS plus Ph.D. Subject_____(6.3)
_____Master's degree, not in library science(6.4)
_____Other:_____(6.5)
```

7. How many professional journals do you read at least every other issue?

```
_____Journals read
```

8. How many professional journals do you scan at least every other issue?

```
_____Journals scanned
```

9. How many state and national library or information science conferences have you attended during the last three years?

```
_____State (9.1)
_____National (9.2)
_____Other (9.3)
```

10. How many formal workshops, continuing education courses or other organized professional development activities have you attended during the last three years?

```
-----Workshops(10.1)
------Courses   (10.2)
------Other     (10.3)
```

11. How many professional and scholarly associations are you a member of? Please count each division of A.L.A. as a separate association.

```
------Associations
```

12. How many separate committee assignments or elected positions have you held in professional and scholarly associations during the last three years?

```
------Assignments or positions
```

13. How many separate university committee assignments have you held during the last three years? Include both appointive and elective positions.

```
------Assignments
```

14. How many papers have you presented before professional or scholarly associations or had published, either in book, chapter or journal article form, in the last five years?

```
------Papers
```

15. On how many occasions in the last five years have you served as panel participant or moderator at professional meetings?

```
------Participant(15.1)
------Moderator(15.2)
```

Appendix A1 (*Continued*)

16. What is the approximate Full Time Equivalent student enrollment of your college/university?

-----10,000 or fewer (16.1)
-----10,001 to 20,000(16.2)
-----20,001 to 30,000(16.3)
-----30,001 or more (16.4)

17. What was your total library operations budget, including personnel, books, periodicals, supplies and services, and equipment, during the 1983-84 fiscal year?

18. What were the approximate percentages of library operations budget support in 1983-84 from each of these sources?

-----% from college/university funds (18.1)
-----% from grants, contracts, gifts (18.2)
-----% from separate endowment (18.3)

19. What is the principal source of college/university financial support?

-----Public (state, city, county or other governmental) funds.(19.1)
-----Private (tuition, church, foundation, endowment) funds. (19.2)

THANK YOU FOR YOUR PARTICIPATION IN THE LEADER ACTIVITY STUDY!

Leader Activity Study Questionnaire, Constituents

LEADER ACTIVITY STUDY

These statements refer to the activities a manager might or might not perform, depending on individual circumstances. You are asked to indicate how effective the library chief executive on your campus is in carrying out these activities. You may not have direct knowledge of some activities; in those cases, please respond to the best of your knowledge.

In answering, use the following scale and place the appropriate number in the blank space to the left of each statement.

EFFECTIVENESS

1	2	3	4	5
Not at all	Somewhat	Moderately	Quite	Extremely

Example:

1. Running departmental meetings.

BE SURE to answer every item. Do not skip any. Where you are not sure, answer to the best of your knowledge or judgment.

128

_____ 1. Evaluating subordinate job performance.

_____ 2. Initiating new ideas for services and/or operations.

_____ 3. Planning and implementing changes in the library.

_____ 4. Distributing budgeted resources.

_____ 5. Integrating subordinates' goals (e.g. career goals and work preferences) with the university's and library's goals and objectives.

_____ 6. Forwarding important information to subordinates.

_____ 7. Attending social functions inside the library and the university to keep up contacts.

_____ 8. Keeping up with professional trends and changes that might have an impact on the library.

_____ 9. Serving as an expert or providing advice to people outside of the library.

_____ 10. Initiating controlled change in the library.

_____ 11. Making decisions about time parameters for upcoming programs.

_____ 12. Directing the work of subordinates.

_____ 13. Allocating human resources to specific jobs or tasks.

129

Appendix A2 *(Continued)*

_____ 14. Attending conferences or meetings of other groups or organizations.

_____ 15. Keeping up with information on the progress of programs and operations throughout the library and the university.

_____ 16. Keeping others informed of the library's future plans.

_____ 17. Solving problems by instituting needed changes in the library.

_____ 18. Preventing the loss or threat of loss of human or capital resources valued by the library.

_____ 19. Resolving conflicts between subordinates.

_____ 20. Keeping track of subordinates' training and special skills as they relate to job assignments--so as to facilitate their personal growth and development.

_____ 21. Attending social functions as a representative of the library.

_____ 22. Keeping up with technological developments related to the library and the university.

_____ 23. Answering letters or inquiries on behalf of the library.

_____ 24. Allocating monies within the library.

_____ 25. Giving negative feedback by criticizing subordinates' actions when appropriate.

26. Scanning the external environment for new opportunities to improve services or operations.

27. Serving on committees and/or task forces as a representative of the library.

28. Providing other people with information about the library's activities and plans.

29. Deciding which programs to provide resources to (human resources, materials, dollars, equipment, etc.)

30. Seeing to it that subordinates are alert to problems that need attention.

31. Staying attuned to the informal communication networks.

32. Gatherng information about library users, other units of the university, new professional developments.

33. Allocating equipment or materials.

34. Using his/her authority to insure that subordinates accomplish important tasks.

35. Touring facilities or work stations for observational purposes.

36. Developing contacts with important people outside the library.

37. Learning about new ideas originating outside the library.

Appendix A2 (*Continued*)

38. Providing new employees with adequate training for and introduction to the job at hand.

39. Reading reports on activities in the library and other units in the university.

40. Obtaining adequate resources to administer library service programs and build library collections.

Methodological Notes

SCORE COMPUTATION

Index scores were constructed for each of the three principal dimensions: leader activity, reputational effectiveness, and changes in organizational domain.

Leader Activity

Mean individual scores for the 42 directors were computed for each of the six managerial roles, averaged for the 42 leaders, and used for comparisons with reputational effectiveness ratings. In order to make a sharper distinction between high and low activity leaders, a second set of "high activity frequency scores" was computed based on the frequency with which the leaders indicated that they performed a given activity at the "4" ("To a considerable extent") or "5" ("To an extreme extent") level. The frequency of these responses was divided by the number of activity items making up each role so that comparisons among managerial roles could be made. The sum of all "4" and "5" responses was used as the index of overall leader activity.

Reputational Effectiveness

Reputational effectiveness scores were computed by the same methods as were Leader Activity Scores, except that all raw scores were also normalized by dividing them by the number of constituents for each leader case.

Domain Management

The amount of reported organizational change during the preceding five years or during the leader's tenure in the position, whichever was shorter, was adopted as the measure of domain management. Responses were simple yes/no replies to a list of 34 potential changes. Raw change scores were normalized by dividing the reported number of changes by years in position, up to a maximum of five years.

EIGHT LEADERSHIP TYPES

Description of a director as high or low on each dimension is based on placement in the total array of scores. The array of scores on each index was treated as an objective scale from the lowest score for the study population to the highest, and the average of the lowest and highest scores computed as the middle position on the scale. The entire population of leaders was arranged into high/low categories on each index by locating individual scores above or below the midpoint for range of scores. Sixty-nine percent of the focal leaders fell into the high group on the reputational effectiveness index, 28.6 percent on the domain management index, and 45.2 percent on the leader activity index.

Based on the high/low designations, each focal leader was then placed into one of the eight possible combinations of the two ratings on each of the three dimensions.

If the 42 leaders were equally distributed among the eight cells of the final type array, the expected value of each cell would be 5.25. Instead, the results varied considerably from the expected values:

Type I	(HHH)	N = 6
Type II	(HHL)	N = 3
Type III	(HLH)	N = 9
Type IV	(HLL)	N = 11
Type V	(LHH)	N = 1
Type VI	(LHL)	N = 2
Type VII	(LLH)	N = 3
Type VIII	(LLL)	N = 7

A chi-square procedure was performed on the eight types in relation to the three dimensions, and the differences in distribution of types were found to be significant at the .001 level. Additionally, two-way chi-square procedures were performed for each pair of dimensions. Distributions of high/low combinations of reputational effectiveness and leader activity were found to be significant at the .01 level, leader activity and organizational change at the .01 level, and reputational effectiveness and organizational change at the .001 level.

Based on the chi-square significance levels, there is a strong presumption that the eight leader types are separate and distinct for the three dimensions. Because of the small numbers of individuals represented in cells II (HHL), V (LHH), VI (LHL), and VII (LLH), further analysis was limited to the four cells in which the observed incidence of cases exceeded the expected incidence based on uniform distribution.

Bibliography

Aldrich, Howard E. *Organizations and Environments*. Englewood Cliffs, N.J.: Prentice-Hall, 1979.

Anderson, Dorothy J. "Comparative Career Profiles of Academic Librarians: Are Leaders Different?" *The Journal of Academic Librarianship* 10 (1984):326-332.

Baldridge, J. Victor, and Robert Z. Burnham. "Organizational Innovation: Individual, Organizational, and Environmental Impacts." *Administrative Science Quarterly* 20 (1975):165-176.

Barnard, Chester I. *The Functions of the Executive*. Cambridge, Mass.: Harvard University Press, 1938.

Bavelas, A. "Leadership: Man and Function." In B. M. Staw (ed.), *Psychological Foundations of Organizational Behavior*. Santa Monica, Calif.: Goodyear Publishing Co., 1977, pp. 324-329.

Baysinger, Barry D. "Domain Maintenance as an Objective of Business Political Activity: An Expanded Typology." *Academy of Management Review* 9 (1984):248-258.

Bennis, W. G. "Leadership Theory and Administrative Behavior: The Problems of Authority." *Administrative Science Quarterly* 4 (1959):259-301.

——. *The Leaning Ivory Tower*. San Francisco: Jossey-Bass, 1973.

——, and Burt Nanus. *Leaders: The Strategies for Taking Charge*. New York: Harper and Row, 1985.

Berlew, D. E. "Leadership and Organizational Excitement." In B. M. Staw (ed.), *Psychological Foundations of Organizational Behavior*.

Santa Monica, Calif.: Goodyear Publishing Co., 1977, pp. 329-343.

———, and D. T. Hall. "The Socialization of Managers: Effects of Expectations on Performance." *Administrative Science Quarterly* 11 (1966):207-223.

Blake, R. R., and J. S. Mouton. *The Managerial Grid III: The Key to Leadership Excellence*. Houston, Tex.: Gulf Publishing Co., 1985.

Blalock, Hubert M., Jr. *Social Statistics*. New York: McGraw-Hill Book Co., 1960.

Blau, Judith R., and William McKinley. "Idea Complexity and Innovation." *Administrative Science Quarterly* 24 (1979):200-219.

Buckland, Michael K. *Library Services in Theory and Context*. New York: Pergamon Press, 1983.

Burke, W. W. "Review of Leadership: Where Else Can We Go?" *Journal of Applied Behavioral Sciences* 15 (1979):121-122.

Burns, James McGregor. *Leadership*. New York: Harper and Row, 1978.

Cameron, Kim, and David A. Whetten. "Organizational Effectiveness: One Model or Several?" In K. Cameron and D. Whetten (eds.), *Organizational Effectiveness: A Comparison of Multiple Models*. New York: Academic Press, 1983, pp. 1-24.

Campbell, John P. "On the Nature of Organizational Effectiveness." In P. Goodman and J. Pennings (eds.), *New Perspectives on Organizational Effectiveness*. San Francisco: Jossey-Bass, 1977, pp. 13-55.

Child, John. "Organizational Structure, Environment and Performance: The Role of Strategic Choice." *Sociology* 6 (1972):1-22.

Cleveland, Harlan. *The Knowledge Executive*. New York: Truman Talley Books/E. P. Dutton, 1985.

Cooley, C. H. *Human Nature and the Social Order*. New York: Scribner's, 1902.

Cyert, Richard M., and James G. March. *A Behavioral Theory of the Firm*. Englewood Cliffs, N.J.: Prentice-Hall, 1963.

Daft, Richard L. "A Dual Core Model of Organizational Innovation." *Academy of Management Journal* 21 (1978):193-210.

Deal, Terrence E., and Allen A. Kennedy. *Corporate Cultures: The Rites and Rituals of Corporate Life*. Reading, Mass.: Addison-Wesley Publishing Co., 1982.

De Gennaro, R. "Library Administration and New Management Systems." *Library Journal* (December 15, 1978):2477-2482.

Dewar, Robert D., and Robert B. Duncan. "Implications for Organizational Design of Structural Alteration as a Consequence of Growth and Innovation." *Organization and Administrative Science* 8 (1977):203-222.

Dill, William R. "Environment as an Influence on Managerial Autonomy." *Administrative Science Quarterly* 2 (1958):409-443.

Dragon, A. C. "Leader Behavior in Changing Libraries." In C. McClure and A. R. Samuels (eds.), *Strategies for Library Administration: Concepts and Approaches*. Littleton, Colo.: Libraries Unlimited, 1982, pp. 96-109.

Drucker, Peter F. "Managing the Public Service Institution." *The Public Interest* 33 (Fall 1973):43-60.

Euster, Joanne R. "The Activities and Effectiveness of the Academic Library Director in the Environmental Context." Ph.D. diss., University of California-Berkeley, 1986.

Fayol, H. *General and Industrial Management*. London: Pitman, 1949.

Fleishman, E. "The Measurement of Leadership Attitudes in Industry." *Journal of Applied Psychology* 37 (1953):153-158.

———, E. F. Harris, and H. E. Burtt. *Leadership and Supervision in Industry*. Columbus, Ohio: Bureau of Educational Research, Ohio State University, 1955.

Frankie, S. O. "Occupational Characteristics of University Librarianship: A Study of the Values, Behavioral Styles and Work Preferences of University Catalog and Reference Librarians." Paper presented at Association of College and Research Libraries National Conference, Minneapolis, Minn., October 1981.

Gaertner, Gregory H., and S. Ramnarayan. "Organizational Effectiveness: an Alternative Perspective." *Academy of Management Review* 8 (1983):97-107.

Gardner, John W. *The Tasks of Leadership*. Leadership Papers/2. Washington, D.C.: Leadership Studies Program, Independent Sector, 1986.

Griffin, R. W. "Relationships among Individual, Task Design, and Leader Behavior Variables." *Academy of Management Journal* 23 (1980):665-683.

Hall, J., J. B. Harvey, and M. Williams. *Styles of Management Inventory*. The Woodlands, Tex.: Teleometrics International, 1980.

Hannan, Michael T., and John Freeman. "Obstacles to Comparative Studies." In P. Goodman and J. Pennings (eds.), *New Perspectives in Organizational Effectiveness*. San Francisco: Jossey-Bass, 1977, pp. 106-131.

Hills, Frederick S., and Thomas A. Mahoney. "University Budgets and Organizational Decision-making." *Administrative Science Quarterly* 23 (1978):454-465.

Hirschman, Albert O. *Exit, Voice, and Loyalty*. Cambridge, Mass.: Harvard University Press, 1970.

Hollander, E. P. "Competence and Conformity in the Acceptance of

Influence." *Journal of Abnormal and Social Psychology* 61 (1960):365-369.

———. "Emergent Leadership and Social Influence." In L. Petrullo and B. M. Chase (eds.), *Leadership and Interpersonal Behavior*. New York: Holt, Rinehart and Winston, 1961, pp. 30-47.

Holmes, Richard C. "The Academic Library Director's Perceived Power and Its Correlates." Ph.D. diss., University of Minnesota, 1983.

House, R. J. "A 1976 Theory of Charismatic Leadership." In J. G. Hunt and L. L. Larson, *Leadership, the Cutting Edge*. Carbondale: Southern Illinois University Press, 1977, p. 189-207.

———. "A Path-Goal Theory of Leader Effectiveness." *Administrative Science Quarterly* 16 (1971):321-338.

———, and M. L. Baetz. "Leadership: Some Empirical Generalizations and New Research Directions." *Research in Organizational Behavior* 1 (1979):341-423.

Howard, Helen A. "Organizational Structure and Innovation in Academic Libraries." *College and Research Libraries* 42 (1981): 425-434.

Kahn, Robert. "Organizational Effectiveness: An Overview." In P. Goodman and J. Pennings (eds.), *New Perspectives on Organizational Effectiveness*. San Francisco: Jossey-Bass, 1977, pp. 235-248.

Katz, Daniel, Barbara A. Gutek, Robert L. Kahn, and Eugenia Benton. *Bureaucratic Encounters: A Pilot Study in the Evaluation of Government Services*. Ann Arbor: Survey Research Center, Institute for Social Research, University of Michigan, 1975.

Katz, Daniel, and Robert L. Kahn. *The Social Psychology of Organizations*. New York: John Wiley and Sons, 1966.

———. *The Social Psychology of Organizations*. 2d ed. New York: John Wiley and Sons, 1978.

Lieberson, S., and J. F. O'Connor. "Leadership and Organizational Performance: A Study of Large Corporations." *American Sociological Review* 37 (1972):117-130.

Lombardo, M. M., and M. W. McCall, Jr. "Leaders on the Line: Observations From a Simulation of Managerial Work." In J. G. Hunt, U. Sekaran, and C. A. Schriesheim (eds.), *Leadership: Beyond Establishment Views*. Carbondale: Southern Illinois University Press, 1982.

Lynch, Beverly P. "The Academic Library and Its Environment." *College and Research Libraries* 35 (1974):126-132.

McAnally, Arthur M., and Robert B. Downs. "The Changing Role of Directors of University Libraries." *College and Research Libraries* 34 (1973):103-125.

McCall, M. W., Jr., and C. A. Segrist. *In Pursuit of the Manager's Job:*

Building on Mintzberg. Greensboro, N.C.: Center for Creative Leadership, 1980.

McClelland, D. C., S. Rhinesmith, and R. Kristensen. "The Effects of Power Training on Community Action Agencies." *Journal of Applied Behavioral Science* 11 (1975):92-115.

McClure, C. R. *Information for Academic Decision Making: The Case for Organizational Information Management.* Westport, Conn.: Greenwood Press, 1980a.

———. "Library Managers: Can They Manage? Will They Lead?" *Library Journal* (November 15, 1980b), 2388-2391.

Maccoby, Michael. *The Leader.* New York: Simon and Schuster, 1981.

March, James G., and Herbert A. Simon, *Organizations.* New York: John Wiley and Sons, 1958.

Marchant, M. P. "An Open System Theory Approach to Library Effectiveness." In *Library Effectiveness: A State of the Art.* Chicago: Library Administration and Management Association/American Library Association, 1980, pp. 151-154.

———.*Participative Management in Academic Libraries.* Westport, Conn.: Greenwood Press, 1976.

Martell, C. "Administration: Which Way—Traditional Practice or Modern Theory?" *College and Research Libraries* 33 (1972):104-112.

———. *The Client-Centered Academic Library.* Westport, Conn.: Greenwood Press, 1983.

Meyer, John W., and Brian Rowan. "Institutionalized Organizations: Formal Structure as Myth and Ceremony." *American Journal of Sociology* 83 (1977):340-363.

Meyer, M. W. "Leadership and Organizational Structure." *American Journal of Sociology* 81 (1975):514-542.

Miles, Raymond E. *Theories of Management: Implications for Organizational Behavior and Development.* New York: McGraw-Hill Book Company, 1975.

———, Charles C. Snow, and Jeffrey Pfeffer. "Organization—Environment: Concepts and Issues." *Industrial Relations* 13 (1974):244-264.

Mintzberg, H. "If You're Not Serving Bill and Barbara, Then You're Not Serving Leadership." In J. G. Hunt, U. Sekaran, and C. A. Schriesheim (eds.), *Leadership: Beyond Establishment Views.* Carbondale: Southern Illinois University Press, 1982.

———. *The Nature of Managerial Work.* New York: Harper and Row, 1973.

Moch, Michael K. "Structure and Organizational Resource Allocation." *Administrative Science Quarterly* 21 (1976):661-674.

————, and Edward V. Morse. "Size, Centralization and Organizational Adoption of Innovations." *American Sociological Review* 43 (1977):716-725.

Mohr, Lawrence B. "The Implications of Effectiveness Theory for Managerial Practice in the Public Sector." In K. Cameron and D. Whetten (eds.), *Organizational Effectiveness: A Comparison of Multiple Models*. New York: Academic Press, 1983, pp. 225-239.

Moran, Barbara B. *Academic Libraries: The Changing Knowledge Centers of Colleges and Universities*. ASHE-ERIC Higher Education Research Report no. 8. Washington, D.C.: Association for the Study of Higher Education, 1984.

Morrison, A. W., M. W. McCall, Jr., and D. L. De Vries. *Feedback to Managers: A Comprehensive Review of Twenty-four Instruments*. Greensboro, N.C.: Center for Creative Leadership, 1978.

Naisbitt, John, and Patricia Aburdence. *Reinventing the Corporation*. New York: Warner Books, 1985.

Nance, Richard E. "Strategic Simulation of a Library/User/Funder System." Ph.D. diss., Purdue University, 1968.

Newman, William H., and Harvey W. Wallender III. "Managing Not-for-profit Enterprises." *Academy of Management Review* 3 (1978):24-31.

Nie, Norman H., et al. *SPSS: Statistical Package for the Social Sciences*. 2d ed. New York: McGraw-Hill Book Company, 1975.

Ouchi, W. G. *Theory Z.: How American Business Can Meet the Japanese Challenge*. Reading, Mass.: Addison-Wesley Publishing Co., 1981.

Pennings, Johannes M., and Paul S. Goodman. "Toward a Workable Framework." In P. Goodman and J. Pennings (eds.), *New Perspectives on Organizational Effectiveness*. San Francisco: Jossey-Bass, 1977, pp. 146-184.

Person, Ruth J. "Middle Managers in Academic and Public Libraries: Managerial Role Concepts." Ph.D. diss., University of Michigan, 1980.

Peters, Thomas J., and Robert H. Waterman, Jr. *In Search of Excellence: Lessons from America's Best-Run Companies*. New York: Harper and Row, 1982.

Pfeffer, J. "The Ambiguity of Leadership." *Academy of Management Review* 2 (1977):104-112.

————. "Management as Symbolic Action: The Creation and Maintenance of Organizational Paradigms." *Research in Organizational Behavior* 3 (1981):1-52.

————. "Size and Composition of Corporate Boards of Directors: The

Organization and Its Environment." *Administrative Science Quarterly* 17 (1972):218-228.

———. "Size, Composition and Function of Hospital Boards of Directors: A Study of Environment Linkage." *Administrative Science Quarterly* 18 (1973):349-364.

———. "Usefulness of the Concept." In P. Goodman and J. Pennings (eds.), *New Perspectives on Organizational Effectiveness*. San Francisco: Jossey-Bass, 1977, pp. 132-145.

———, and William L. Moore. "Power in University Budgeting: A Replication and Extension." *Administrative Science Quarterly* 25 (1980):637-653.

———, and Gerald R. Salancik. "Administrator Effectiveness: The Effects of Advocacy and Information on Achieving Outcomes in an Organizational Context." *Human Relations* 30 (1977):641-656.

———. "Determinants of Supervisory Behavior: A Role Set Analysis." *Human Relations* 28 (1975):139-154.

———. *The External Control of Organizations: A Resource Dependence Perspective*. New York: Harper and Row, 1978.

———. "Organizational Decision Making as a Political Process: The Case of the University Budget." *Administrative Science Quarterly* 19 (1974):135-151.

Pickle, Hal, and Frank Friedlander. "Seven Societal Criteria of Organizational Success." *Personnel Psychology* 20 (1968):165-178.

Podsakoff, P. M., W. D. Todor, and R. Skov. "Effects of Leader Contingent and Noncontingent Reward and Punishment Behaviors on Subordinate Performance and Satisfaction." *Academy of Management Journal* 25 (1982):810-821.

Pondy, Louis R., and Ian I. Mitroff. "Beyond Open System Models of Organization." *Research in Organizational Behavior* 1 (1979):3-39.

Rainey, Hal G., R. W. Backoff, and C. H. Lewis. "Comparing Public and Private Organizations." *Public Administration Review* 36 (1976):233-244.

Rice, A. K. *The Enterprise and Its Environment*. London: Tavistock Publications, 1963.

Salancik, G. R. "Leadership as an Outcome of Social Structure and Process." In J. G. Hunt and L. L. Larson (eds.), *Leadership Frontiers*. Kent, Ohio: Comparative Administrative Research Institute, Kent State University, 1975.

Sayles, L. R. *Managerial Behavior: Administration in Complex Organizations*. New York: McGraw-Hill Book Co., 1964.

Schneider, Benjamin. "An Interactionist Perspective on Organizational Effectiveness." In K. Cameron and D. Whetten (eds.), *Organizational Effectiveness, a Comparison of Multiple Models.* New York: Academic Press, 1983, pp. 27-54.

Scott, W. Richard. "Effectiveness of Organizational Effectiveness Studies." In P. Goodman and J. Pennings (eds.), *New Perspectives on Organizational Effectiveness.* San Francisco: Jossey-Bass, 1977, pp. 63-95.

Seashore, Stanley E. "A Framework for an Integrated Model of Organizational Effectiveness." In K. Cameron and D. Whetten (eds.), *Organizational Effectiveness: A Comparison of Multiple Models.* New York: Academic Press, 1983, pp. 55-70.

Shoham, Snunith. *Organizational Adaptation by Public Libraries.* Westport, Conn.: Greenwood Press, 1984.

Siegel, Signey. *Nonparametric Statistics for the Behavioral Sciences.* New York: McGraw-Hill Book Co., 1956.

Sparks, R. "Library Management: Consideration and Structure." *The Journal of Academic Librarianship* 2 (1976):66-71.

Stewart, R. "The Relevance of Some Studies of Managerial Work and Behavior to Leadership Research." In J. G. Hunt, U. Sekaran, and C. A. Schriesheim (eds.), *Leadership: Beyond Establishment Views.* Carbondale: Southern Illinois University Press, 1982, pp. 11-30.

Stogdill, R. M. *Handbook of Leadership: A Survey of Theory and Research.* New York: The Free Press, 1974.

———. "Personal Factors Associated with Leadership: A Survey of the Literature." *Journal of Psychology* 25 (1948):35-71.

———. *Stogdill's Handbook of Leadership.* Revised and expanded by Bernard M. Bass. New York: The Free Press, 1981.

Strand, Rich. "A Systems Paradigm of Organizational Adaptations to the Social Environment." *Academy of Management Review* 8 (1983):90-96.

Thompson, James D. *Organizations in Action.* New York: McGraw-Hill Book Co., 1967.

———, and William J. McEwen. "Organizational Goals and Environment: Goal-Setting as an Interaction Process." *American Sociological Review* 23 (1958):23-31.

Tsui, Anne S. "A Multiple Constituency Approach to Managerial Effectiveness: A Theoretical Framework and an Exploratory Study." Ph.D. diss., University of California, Los Angeles, 1981.

———. "The Quality of Managerial Performance Ratings from Multiple Raters: Some Extended and Critical Findings." Unpublished paper, 1984b.

————. "A Role Set Analysis of Managerial Reputation." *Organizational Behavior and Human Performance* 34 (1984a):64-96.

————, and Kirk R. Karwan. "Managerial Effectiveness and Organizational Performance: A Test of Causality." Unpublished paper, March 1984.

Vroom, V. H. "Leadership Revisited." In B. M. Staw (ed.), *Psychological Foundations of Organizational Behavior*. Santa Monica, Calif.: Goodyear Publishing Co., 1977, pp. 343-355.

Watkins, Beverly T. "Critics Say Colleges Do a Poor Job of Developing Leadership Qualities in Their Undergraduates." *The Chronicle of Higher Education* 32 (May 28, 1986):19-40.

Weber, M. *The Theory of Social and Economic Organization*. New York: Oxford University Press, 1947.

Weick, Karl E. "Educational Organizations as Loosely Coupled Systems." *Administrative Science Quarterly* 21 (1976):1-19.

————, and Richard L. Daft. "The Effectiveness of Interpretation Systems." In K. Cameron and D. Whetten (eds.), *Organizational Effectiveness: A Comparison of Multiple Models*. New York: Academic Press, 1983, pp. 71-93.

Whetten, David. "Managing for Effectiveness during Times of Scarcity." Unpublished paper delivered at American Association for Higher Education meeting, Chicago, March 15, 1984.

White, Herbert S. "The Use and Misuse of Library Studies." *Library Journal* 110 (1985):70-71.

Zaltman, Gerald, Robert Duncan, and Jonny Holbek. *Innovations and Organizations*. New York: John Wiley and Sons, 1973.

Index

About the Author

JOANNE R. EUSTER is University Librarian at Rutgers University. She has had many years of experience in college and university library management, and was honored with dissertation and fellowship awards for the study on which this book is based. Her other publications include studies and journal articles on library communications systems, management, and organization.